Unpacking *the* Attic

Also by Ann Mracek

Friendship Flies the Sun

My Best Friends Live in the Woods

FREE OFFER

The recipes mentioned in the book are available at

https://annmracek.com

Praise for Unpacking the Attic

"*Unpacking the Attic* allowed me to replay and repair some of the tapes I had been given as a child. It helped me to forgive and forget. I treat patients' physical trauma every day. This book effectively treats emotional trauma, the other half of health. I will recommend it to all my patients."
—Dr. Michael C. Zimmer, Dorsett Chiropractic St Louis

"*Unpacking the Attic* is a heartfelt collection of stories that takes the reader on a journey of self-discovery and healing. A must-read for anyone seeking to foster self-love and authenticity."
—Monica Malone, senior healthcare analyst in the biomedical engineering field

"Ann has graciously opened the window to her soul to show us the path to healing, forgiveness, and acceptance. *Unpacking the Attic* is a reminder to us all to be kind to our current selves, our past selves, and each other."
—Pat Hooper, co-owner ASL Pewter Foundry

"Wonderful book. I loved learning all about Ann's childhood. The stories are both heartbreaking and hilarious. Give yourself time to slowly read through the book so you can enjoy all the beautiful imagery. I think many people could allow their inner child to heal as they read Ann's stories and reflect on their own journey."
—Joy White, music teacher and former student

"This charming and poignant book goes down like a hot cup of healing tea. Its sweetness permeates and will activate your own childhood memories of love, loss, laughter, and trauma that will be clamoring for their own review. By seeing through the eyes of our inner child, healing and forgiveness can wash in warm and clean, clearing away a lifetime of obstacles and ill-suited narratives we have created for ourselves. The author gives some useful exercises to cherish our inner child, too. Loving your inner child can teach you to love all of yourself. A lovely read—entertaining, healing, timely and very relatable!"
—Dani Morre, global tour director

"*Unpacking the Attic* is an engaging and relatable read that vividly paints a world that readers can immerse themselves in. The book's stories are both thought provoking and comforting, offering insights that encourage introspection. Although the narrative is occasionally non-linear, the author's style remains compelling, leaving readers inspired."
—Sampada Costa, Operations manager video game studio

"The author takes you into this beautiful journey of her home where she once lived, and the memories linked to each room and the artifacts in it. The memories span across four generations. It gives glimpses of the heart of a child that one could associate with their own childhood. Her pets take us into a dream world. Throughout the book, the author inspires and showcases the fact that she never settled for less, despite several challenges. Instead, she upskills herself by all means using the resources available. She nurtures her daughter to land in one of the pristine colleges. She turned her bitter experiences into learnings and molded her life into positivity, a much-needed attitude in today's world for a greater inner peace. Her compassion towards her aged parents and the people around showcases the reverence of a child. Great work on your book, Mrs. Ann!"

–D.S. Robert, Product Manager, Technology

"A delightful read that brought both smiles and tears. I wished I'd had this book before I cleaned out my parents' house. It would've given me some tools to cope with the memories once buried then uncovered."

–Connie Thatcher, owner of Dragonfly Kiln Works

"This is a great book about self-healing, starting from childhood to adulthood to beyond. It takes you on a journey of the author's own childhood memories and how she started her self-healing by writing down her experiences growing up and how she gave herself permission to heal. Reading this book it has given me the courage to sit back and really reflect on my childhood and adult life experiences and to be able to dissect and understand both positive and negative experiences to begin giving myself permission to begin my own self-healing process. I love how the author is vulnerable enough to help someone like me to begin my healing process, finding peace from within, being able to move on and live a happy, healthy, and prosperous life."

–Kim Isbell, customer service quality analyst

"A heartfelt spiritual journey of looking back and moving forward. In the busy days of endless to-do lists, it can be easy to forget about what matters to us most. Ann shares her journey with an honesty and sincerity that reaches you deeply and reminds you of little miracles and your inner child."

–Anya Wynne, software developer

A Path To Healing Your Inner Child

Unpacking *the* Attic

Ann M. Mracek

Copyright © 2024 by Ann M. Mracek

All rights reserved. No part of this book may be used or reproduced by any means, graphic, electronic, or mechanical, including photocopying, recording, taping, or by any information storage retrieval system without the written permission of the author except in the case of brief quotations embodied in critical articles and reviews.

Published by Ann Mracek Publishing

ISBN (paperback): 978-0-9766488-7-1
ISBN (ebook): 978-0-9766488-8-8

Book design and production by www.AuthorSuccess.com

Printed in the United States of America

This is a work of creative nonfiction. The views expressed are solely those of the author, and not meant to treat or cure any illness or disease. All the events in this memoir are true to the best of the author's memory.

Contents

Introduction	1
The Porch Swing—The Place Where It All Began	3
I Remember—Dreams or Time Travel?	6
My Collie Siblings and the Tragic Nap	8
The Playhouse Curtains—Where I Escaped	10
For the Birds—Little Spirits With Wings	13
The Stake—Real or Imaginary?	17
Jacques Michelle—Wait for Me, Will You?	18
Menagerie and the Snake I Wore	21
The Crash—A Lifetime of Pain	24
Bumpy Ride—So Many Angry Words	27
The Wren House—Finding New Purpose	29
Coffee and Ironing—Where Do You Find Joy?	32
Dad's Whistle—Can We Please Talk?	34
The Playhouse—Language of Love	36
Trees—Rooted in My Heart	38
Maui—You Always Understand What I Need Most	41
Did I Tell You About the Turtle?	44
My First Dance Class Was Almost My Last	46
Timeline—So How Did That Work?	50
Liquid Soap Jars—The Grace of Acceptance	52
Why Belly Dance?—The Time I Almost Froze to Death	55
A Bit Of History and the Ghost Who Loves Me	59
Pop—The Grandfather Who Never Talked to Me	62
I Quit—And in So Doing, I Won	65

Trophies—Time to Let Go	67
Big Shot and Gladis—We Must Learn to Fly	70
The Christmas Tree—Making up for Lost Time	75
Augusta—Toxic on So Many Levels	78
The Apple Fridge—And Yet it Persevered	82
Melody—First There Were Many, Then One, Then None	85
The Doctor's Note—I Was Finally Heard	87
The Robberies—Visions of the Future	90
My First Angel Drove Me Home	94
The Back up Angel Found My Keys	97
Red Flyer—A Portal	100
We Hear What We Know	102
The Garden—It's Not What You Think	104
Cloud Spaceships and Betrayal	106
The Scar—Even This Can Heal	109
Auras I Massaged	111
Oatmeal—Life Needs Spice	114
The Pine Tree That Nearly Killed My Father	116
The Green Cake—My Inspiration	119
Pianos—The Focal Point of My Existence	123
Daylilies—Abundance and Resilience	128
New Christmas Reality—And So We Adapt	131
Happiness—Listen to Your Spirit Guides	135
She Cut Her Hair—Manifest Reality	140
The Mink Coat—I've Come a Long Way	143
Slippers—Three Pairs, Three Journeys	146
Parting Thoughts	152
Acknowledgments	*154*

Introduction

I would like to invite you on a journey, not to exotic distant lands, but to the shadows of the past. A journey to the inner landscape of shifting memories where childhood traumas and limiting beliefs need to finally be stared down and healed. There will be giggles and tears, and ultimately the empowerment of forgiveness, insight, and acceptance of loving the child we were, of sending back in time comforting reassurance. There is a path for healing your inner child. Walk down it with me.

I found myself at a crossroads in life. After fifty-six years in their home, my parents suddenly announced that they were moving into an assisted living apartment the following week. The house had to be emptied. They refused to sell anything. They were determined to find a new home for every piece of furniture and give it all away. We bought round sticker dots of green, blue, and orange. The things going to the folks' apartment had a green dot, things my daughter wanted to move to her new house had a blue dot, and a very few things I wanted to move to my house had an orange dot. After that, word went out to all family and friends: if you can haul it off you can have it. The locusts descended, and in two weeks all the furniture was gone. This was a three-story, six-thousand-square-foot house. That is a lot of furniture. But more than furniture, there were closets and cabinets full to the brim of stuff. Somehow, in handling these things and either bringing them to my home, giving them to friends, or donating them, a flood of memories cascaded over me and found their way onto the paper. It was as if these things of my past had stored energy that was washing over me. I remembered the woods when I brought my dad's old thermos bottle out of the pantry. I remembered the turtle when I came across two cartons of Epsom salt in the basement, and so it goes. It was five weeks of moving my parents and unpacking them and emptying and cleaning the house. All of this tumbled out while sitting at the old house while supervising movers or cleaning crews, or at my own dining room table, usually from midnight to the wee hours of the morning, when the house was quiet and I was alone to zone out into my musings. It was a season of reflection. I needed to pause and look back before I could be ready to move forward. I believe our modern world does not value or leave time for retrospection, and I believe that can be a valuable healing elixir.

Memories and truth are like shadows; images in shades of grey. And while they take their shape from the original, their form shifts and distorts as time, distance, and perspectives change. Shown only a shadow, it's often difficult to guess at the true source, and it's up to us to fill in the details as best we can.

It has been my life in review, akin to a near-death experience, but without the dying part, which is darn convenient. It also afforded me the opportunity to send love and acceptance back in time to the often lonely and frightened child I was and to heal and forgive. The creative adult is the child within that survived. Hurt people, hurt people. Healed people, heal people. I invite you to pause and reflect on your own inner child as we embark on this journey together.

Why I write: The siren's call of purpose.

The Porch Swing—The Place Where It All Began

I wanted something to do while I sat on the porch swing and watched the movers clean out my childhood home, and writing this book seemed to jump into my hand. I am forced to remember and reflect as things from my long-forgotten childhood are carried into the light for the last time out of the attic. The doll furniture I played with, the tiny table and two chairs that I sat at with Teddy occupying the second chair. I never got the sister I so desperately wanted. Teddy did his best.

I'm sitting on the porch swing, probably for the last time. It too will be carried away with the rubbish. It's rusted and the front board had to be replaced. It glares back in its newness compared to its weathered compatriots. I made this swing when my daughter was about nine months old for my "old" house of thirty years ago. No, thirty-two years ago. I painted each wooden slat with six coats of polyurethane, brush in my right hand, baby on my left arm and hip. It moved to this house, my parents' house, almost eighteen years ago. I think I look as tired and weathered as it does. We have been left out to weather many storms together, and yet I'm not sad to see it go. Not really. It fulfilled its calling and was enjoyed for many long afternoons of breezes and sunshine. I wonder if I will ever fulfill my own calling. Its siren call has certainly led me down the path of many wonderous pursuits. I wonder just what that calling might be. If it is calling, I apparently am in need of a hearing aid. Perhaps they have been dialing the wrong number all these years? Does anyone actually dial anymore? Kids now don't even know that phones used to have round dials that turned. Or records that turned. Hmmm . . .

As I sit and gently swing, I look out on the front yard. I would say front lawn, but there is no grass. I planted it all in ivy and perennial garden flowers, periwinkle, hosta, astilbe, columbine, daffodils, grape hyacinth, lily of the valley, and Mayapples to name a few. Some I have forgotten the names of. It's a carefree carpet of flowers in the spring. Will the new owners tear them up by the roots? That would make me sad. I've cared for them all for so long. I probably should not come back to see after it's sold; best to remember them thriving and alive. I hope someone will remember me that way someday.

All the furniture is gone. All carried away for new lives in someone else's house. That is good. It's nice to imagine it being used, still needed and appreciated. We all want to be needed and appreciated.

I am amazed at how incredibility dirty the house is now. Was all that really under the furniture? Really? "Thank you, God, for a strong immune system. Amen."

I'll have to leave soon to go teach my evening's worth of piano lessons. I like what I do. I like the idea of passing the torch of music to another generation.

I had a strange encounter today. One of the men moving out junk introduced himself as one of my former students. He is a grown man, but as soon as he said, "It's Corry. You used to teach me piano," I had a mental flash of a little boy of seven with that impish grin and turned up nose trying to find the melody we both knew was in there somewhere.

Just a flash, but as real as I'm standing here. Are all of our memories tucked away that vividly, to be recalled in a next life? That would be good and bad for certain. He says he still enjoys playing now and again. I wonder. Did I add joy to his life? I hope so. Some students more than others, of course.

That flash of memory, seeing him as a child, suddenly enabled me to see another child from the distant past. Myself. Feelings of loneliness, sadness, and rejection welled up from some dark repressed place, and I decided to open that door. To love that little girl who was once me. To embark on an epic journey to heal the child within.

Dreams and time travel could be the same thing . . .

I Remember—Dreams or Time Travel?

I remember lying in bed in this old back bedroom that was once mine. I remember dreaming a train was coming through the room, only to awaken startled and hear the loudest snoring ever emitted from a nose coming out of my dad in the next room.

I remember a night terror when a giant bird of prey would crash through the bedroom window without breaking the glass: a repeating dream that would cause me to cry out. I'd awaken to the huge crash of Dad bouncing off the hall closet door and appearing in my room in a single bound to attack my assailant. He always won. The bird has yet to carry me away.

I remember waking up cold one night, and Dad getting his old army blanket out to add another layer of coziness. But I went into dreams of a train ride at night in Korea, with a woman holding a chicken next to me, and looking down at the filthy floor to see huge boots on my feet. I told Dad, and he hastily removed the blanket. I've never seen it since. He fought in Korea, and it seemed I had tapped into one of his memories. He said best I do not get any more of those. How odd. I still shake my head and say, "How odd."

I REMEMBER—DREAMS OR TIME TRAVEL?

What Dad did not do was comfort the frightened and confused child, so I will do that now. I will stroke back her strawberry blonde curls and kiss her forehead to open her third eye. I will say to her, "Embrace your gifts."

I fell asleep on so many nights with the covers over my head, gripped in fear. When those memories return, I focus my heart on everything that makes me laugh. Always try to laugh as you fall asleep. Marinate in that vibration for the next eight hours. Embark on a dream voyage from the dock of joy.

I remember falling asleep with my chemistry book in hand. It was the best cure for insomnia ever.

I remember the Cuckoo Clock on the wall by my headboard. I hated one crow. 12:30, 1:00, 1:30 a.m.? Some things do improve with time. Now I have a lighted projection on the ceiling to tell the time at night; no noisy bird to annoy and tease me. I guess a lot of time has slipped by. If I had kept the Cuckoo Clock wound up, I wonder how many times he would have crowed by now. Do Cuckoos get sore throats? Silly old bird.

Innocent companions are the best and truest comfort.

My Collie Siblings and the Tragic Nap

We had two collie dogs as I grew up. They were the children B.A. (before Ann). My parents tried for nine years to have me. The dogs were old when I was born. I remember crawling into the sweet hay of the doghouse to nap with Debbie. She was so soft and warm. Dad would let me walk around the neighborhood with the dogs, Gent and Debbie. "Just hold on to the leash," he would instruct me.

The dogs would actually be walking me. They would go up the street and then bring me back. I thought I was so "big." We shared hamburgers, ice cream cones, and big wet kisses. One nap was tragic. I woke to a cold, still Debbie. I was so young I didn't know what was wrong with her. Terror gripped me and I ran to Mom. "Something is wrong with Debbie!"

I never saw her again. I didn't get to say goodbye. But that is the best we can all hope for: to drift off peacefully napping in the arms of love. Dad took down the doghouse. Goodbye Debbie.

The experience instilled in me a terror of death.

When I was in my early twenties, my mother's father, Grandad, was losing his battle with cancer. Mom and I drove to Augusta to see him for the last time. As I stood by his hospital bed, his face lit up with the splendor of a vision. He grabbed my hand, and his last words were, "Don't be afraid, it's beautiful."

He died with a smile. Somehow, he knew I held a terror of death.

Now I know that the spirit is eternal and sheds its avatar when it is used up. I will do what my mother failed to do and explain to my inner child that Debbie is forever with me in spirit. That life and death are two sides of the same coin in perfect balance. And I will tell her that Grandad understands and will make it all better. Just be patient, little one. Trust that life and death are both natural and splendid. That time is an illusion, and the infinite loving universe will continue to teach our souls.

*It is not the avatar I see,
but the spirit I feel through the lens of memory.*

~⚜~

The Playhouse Curtains—
Where I Escaped

Now I'm saying goodbye to the backyard, where pets are buried and the playhouse still stands, now with old lawn mowers and fertilizers and a bad smell. It used to be my private world of imagination. I used to plan that I would live there when I got hurt and upset by my parents. My dog and I would just move in. It was my version of running away.

THE PLAYHOUSE CURTAINS—WHERE I ESCAPED

I made curtains for its windows out of old burlap bags. I cut out flowers of felt and sewed them on with pom-pom centers. They still hang there: really faded, falling apart old curtains. But in my mind's eye, I still take pride in them and see them as they were. I hope God will see me as I was in my youth. I sure don't want to spend eternity in a worn out painful wrinkled sack! But I digress.

There were many times I wanted to escape, to run away and hide in the playhouse. The screaming fights of my parents were beyond my understanding except to instill terror in my heart and undermine any feeling of safety. Now, when I recall that time, I allow myself to relive it. These traumas are stored in the body as pain and tension, usually along the body's central core, often in the chest, gut, or solar plexus. Breathe into this pain. You must feel to heal. The energy that has not been felt cannot be released. Place your hand over the body part that is in pain and send love and healing to the child within. When we connect with the body part that is holding that old trauma and send it the love that child deserved and needed, we begin to fix the root cause of so much anxiety we carry into adulthood.

If emotional stress elevates inflammation it translates to chronic disease over time. When you heal these childhood traumas, you are healing the root cause of so many chronic diseases. The body holds trauma on a cellular level.

I never actually ran away, though I tried to plan for it many times. I would lay in bed awake and plot my escape. But the one thing that always blocked me from going was my love of and sense of responsibility for my dog. I could never think of a way to care for and feed him. Carrying that big bag of dog food was a problem, and leaving him behind was not an option. I could not bear the thought of separation, and so my unwavering devotion to his sweet little self was my source of bravery in the face of conflict.

Even now, as I try to stand back and objectively see my inner child, I can smile and be proud. As a child, I could not imagine the danger I could have subjected myself to had I actually run away, but I placed his well-being over my own desires. It was my love for another that kept me safe, and for that I will tell my inner child, "Well done. I'm proud of you."

Just fly away, my darling. Just fly away.

For the Birds—
Little Spirits With Wings

When I was fifty, I developed an allergy to feathers. I had to replace all the pillows and comforters in the house at great aggravation and expense. I gave away my long-down winter coat to be replaced with a man-made poly that has never been as warm. But all that aside, the one treasure I gave away still stings in my memory as a great loss. It had no value except for me. It was the feather collection I had been adding to every summer of my childhood, and even on occasion into adulthood. As I played in the backyard, I would come across the brilliant red of a cardinal feather or the striped blue of a jay and be thrilled and delighted. Each one would be washed, dried, combed, and frozen to preserve, and gently laid in the old shirt box from Famous Barr department store. I had duck feathers from my pet duck Elmer. He had imprinted on me, and we spent a summer playing follow the leader in circles around that backyard. Sadly, Elmer refused to be potty trained, and Mom got tired of washing the front of my blouses that he decorated as I carried him around the yard, so Elmer went back to the farm.

Then there was Fluffy. She was a dappled brown Banny hen. The two poodles we had at the time would gang up on her and pluck out all of her feathers. That silly bird would stand her ground and fight back. She never figured out that she could just fly away; it was always turf wars between her and the dogs. Then, Dad would come home to find her in this sad state of being plucked naked,  grease her up with Vaseline, and keep her in the old baby playpen in the basement until her feathers grew back. After this happened a couple of times, he took pity on her, and she went back to the farm. As a child, I never caught the irony in her name.

I realize as I look back that there are events and even relationships that I am still trying to battle, and I am still holding on to anger and resentment. But I am standing on the empty battlefield of memory, flailing at shadows. The battle is over, and no one has told me. My hurt inner child is still standing her ground. I will tell my child the battle is over. I won. I am an adult now. I give myself permission to spread my wings and fly.

Sometimes we need to learn to just fly away.

But the bird who won all our hearts was Billy. My parents hatched him from an egg. He was a beautiful apple green parakeet. My parents adopted Billy before I was born, so my world had always included this feathered brother.

Billy's cage was a tall rectangle that stood in the corner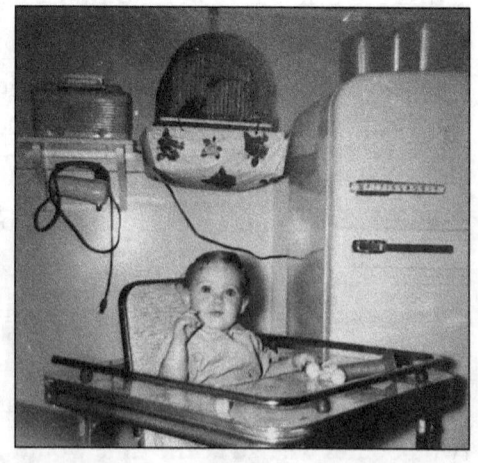

of the kitchen. It had a door that would slide up to open. It was always open and held up with a twisty tie. Billy had free run of the house; or should I say free flight.

My parents used to have contests to see who could teach him to say something new. His repertoire was immense, and he would put his head under the dome of the water bowl and practice talking, like singing in the shower. Among his many sayings were, "I'm Daddy's boy," "I'm a pretty little green parakeet," and "Birdseed tastes lousy."

He would bark like our collies, Gent and Debbie, and ring like the telephone. But the one I liked best was when he would hang on the side of that sliding door, shake it so it rattled and cry, "Help! Let me out!" It was just too funny! Sometimes we imagine we are trapped when the door was open all along!

If ever God gave a bird a spirit, Billy had one. He would sit on the rims of my dad's eyeglasses and bend over to look in his eye, hanging upside down. He would sit on my dad's shoulder, then peck his ear lobe and scamper away. Such a tease.

We would often see Gent or Debbie walk by with Billy perched on their back for the ride. Mush! Gent and Billy were particularly close. Gent was a big white collie with beautiful long chest fur. Gent would lie down and cross his paws in front, and Billy would crawl up on those folded paws and gently groom Gent's chest hairs with his tiny beak. He would make long silky straight rows of the beautiful white fur. Occasionally Gent would lick him, knocking him over with the kiss, and Billy would climb back up and continue the beauty shop treatment.

We learned just how much the dogs loved Billy with the pork roast incident. Billy had always flown around the house at will. Well, one evening, Mom had left the pork roast on the kitchen table to cool in the baking dish. Billy landed in the big rectangular corning dish and marched end to end, hip-deep in the greasy pork gravy! When Dad pulled him out, all his feathers were glued together with grease, and he looked tiny and scrawny. We laughed until we cried. Dad tried to wash him off with dishwashing liquid, but he smelled like a pork chop for weeks. To our amazement, the collies did not try to eat him.

We should always stay open to the possibilities of friendship with those who are completely different than ourselves. Celebrate their uniqueness and love their spirit. My husband and I are avid travelers, which can find us on the other side of the planet in strange and challenging circumstances. When surrounded by strangers, it always serves me best when I smile. When I come from a place of compassion; when I extend the offer of friendship and respect, I can draw on the memory and inspiration from my childhood of a parakeet and collies who were the best of buddies.

I must have had half the box of feathers full of Billy.

We buried him in the backyard, wrapped in blue velvet and sealed in a pickle jar. Dad engraved his name on a large river stone as a head marker. Goodbye Billy. Goodbye yard.

The spirit is free. Wash away any imagined restraint.

The Stake— Real or Imaginary?

In India, there are still places where the elephant is a working animal. Young boys are given a baby elephant to train and work with. It's a marriage of sorts. They will be together until one of them dies; their expected life spans well matched.

When they are small, a steel cuff is placed on the elephant's ankle with a chain staked to a huge, immovable tree. No matter how the little elephant strains against it, she cannot budge. As time and training go on, the size and strength of the stake on the other end of the chain gets smaller, even though the elephant gets bigger and stronger. They are brainwashed into believing that when their ankle is chained to a stake they cannot move. Eventually a two-ton elephant will stand still in one place staked to a twig.

My first marriage was like that. I felt staked down and trapped, when really all I needed to do was walk away.

Sometimes we let ourselves get tricked into believing we are trapped by abuses, addictions, theologies, or anything else that tries to chain us. Try to stand back and assess your situation: is the stake real or imaginary? Are we really being held back, stuck in one place with no freedom to move, or can we clear our assumptions and our minds and just walk forward.

It kind of reminds me of Billy on the cage door.

*Please forgive me when I am gone.
I never meant to leave you.*

Jacques Michelle—
Wait for Me, Will You?

I was an only child. Mom lost many babies in the first trimester, and one after me. I expect I'll have siblings to meet in heaven, but here on Earth I was lonely. So much so that after the collies went to heaven, we got a black miniature poodle named Angel. Poor Angel developed a brain tumor, but she had one litter of puppies: three girls and a boy. The breeder got pick of the litter and thankfully chose a girl. The boy was sent to me from God. From the moment that tiny puppy saw me,

I was his whole world. He followed my every step. He was my constant companion and slept in the crook of my knees for the rest of my childhood. I named him Jacques Michelle. A good French name, and my middle name is Michelle, so it was perfect.

Every secret he heard, every tear he soothed, every joy he shared, every meal I slipped him treats from my plate. Never has there ever been a better match between child and dog than Ann Michelle and Jacques Michelle. He was so desper-  ately needed, and he filled that void so completely. But little girls grow up. My first semester of college I got a phone call from Dad telling me that Jacques had died, I suspected from having a broken heart when I left. I cried for weeks... no months. I still cry sometimes when I think of Jacques Michelle.

Please God, please—let him sleep in the crook of my knee in heaven, or it will not be paradise to me.

Dad said that one night, about a year after Jacques took his place in the backyard next to Billy, a strange warm feeling woke him. There was Jacques, come to say goodbye. I was so torn with conflicting emotions over this. Thrilled to know his spirit is still a vital force, but sad and confused about why didn't he come back to me? Was my dorm room at KU just too hard to find? Did he only know the old house and that yard where we played? Did he come back looking for me to find me still gone? I will try to forgive myself. It was very hard to let the crew carry away his old feeding bowl.

Jacques kept me from running away as a child, and yet, ironically, I did, in fact, leave him behind. Some things in life are hard, but how long am I going to punish myself for growing up? It is time to stand back and forgive myself. Jacques does not blame me, I am sure. His love was unconditional. Doesn't my inner child deserve that same unconditional love?

Loneliness is an undertow, lurking just below a smile.

Menagerie and the Snake I Wore

Being an only child, we always had a menagerie of pets to occupy me. There were turtles in the backyard each summer. We had chameleon lizards in a glass fish tank, and one iguana. The iguana was small and sickly when we got him from the pet store, but with meal worms and lots of fresh produce, he thrived and grew. His color became a brilliant teal blue, and he would swim in the oceans of our bathtub. Seeing him thrive on nutrition and exercise is a lesson I will always remember. We finally took him to the children's zoo, where he had a much bigger cage and lots of children to entertain.

We also once supplied the children's zoo with a screech owl. It was a baby that fell from its nest in that big backyard. We fed it and nursed it, and it grew. All was well, until—one night it let out a scream that peeled the paint off the wall! Hence the name. Who knew?

When I was a child, Dad was gone a lot. He worked nearly every weekend cleaning several acres of woods he had bought as an investment. He would clear lots and rough roads and sell lots for a new subdivision. He had a tractor and a chain saw, and lots of big muscles from his college football scholarship. He learned the names of all of the trees and could identify them all, even in the winter, from the bark. I've always admired that. He passed on his love of trees to me.

One evening, a very tired Daddy came home with a surprise. A tiny magnolia green snake had tapped him on the shoulder in the woods that day. Dad brought home the little snake as our newest pet. Mom was not thrilled, but I was! And of course, it, too, had free run of the house ... or should I say free slither?

It was a fun pet. I would wear it around the house, draped around my neck like a funny boa. At night, it would sleep curled up in Dad's slipper. He had to remember not to put his foot in until the little guy was up in the morning. Mom still was not thrilled, and eventually our now much bigger magnolia green snake joined the others at the children's zoo. Still makes me smile.

I am grateful to my father for bringing home the menagerie and for my mother for tolerating them, even if briefly. I learned to connect with the natural world and gained a profound love for its diverse creatures. We should each examine our hearts. One of the things I am most grateful for is my respect and love for all the creatures of our beautiful Earth. I believe every child is born with the same innate knowing. If your childhood nurtured this connection, rejoice. If not, examine your heart. How can you rekindle this fundamental and essential aspect of your spirit? A long walk in the park? Adopt a pet? Volunteer at an animal shelter? It is essential to know that we are all interconnected. We breathe the same air, drink the same water, and draw our life force from the same spirit.

It's 2 a.m. and I can't sleep. The words are flowing and there is nothing to be done about it except get up and write them down. They are in control.

Tomorrow is the last day of the movers coming to empty the house. Then there will be a cleaning crew, and then the realtor will put a lock box on the front door and dutifully parade perspective buyers through the rooms of my memories. Will the house feel violated, or will it be excited about the chance to have a second life with a new family? What will our ghosts do? Will they move out or adopt a new family?

Push past the pain because you must.
There are no other options.

The Crash—
A Lifetime of Pain

Our realtor grew up in the house next door. She was a few years older than me, so we never really played. I was just the little kid next door, but I always looked at her with marvel. She was so pretty.

One day, as I was playing in the backyard, a bigger boy was climbing up on the neighbor's roof. He shimmied right up the gutter and sat up there all by himself. I asked him why and he said he wanted to be close to my pretty neighbor. That he was sitting above her bedroom window and that was the best place in the world. I don't think I ever told her about that. At the time, I just thought he was a very strange boy. Then, he asked me what I wanted to be when I grew up. Without hesitation I blurted out—"I'm going to be a musician."

He burst into laughter and sang "Kindergarten Baby." Indignant, I said if he didn't want to know he shouldn't have asked. I turned and walked off. And to that I say, "Well done little one!"

His taunt was meant to hurt, but it bounced right off of my confident little self. There has always been an inner knowing of my own worth. When someone shows up on your porch with a box of snakes, don't sign for it! Unless it's a magnolia green snake that likes slippers.

THE CRASH—A LIFETIME OF PAIN

I am a musician; always have been. It's in my DNA. My great uncle was Antonin Dvorak. I have always known I was a musician. I almost flunked kindergarten because of it. There was a piano in the room, and all I wanted to do was learn to play it. The alphabet and numbers held no appeal to me at all. I was so angry and frustrated with my teacher. Why wouldn't she teach me what I wanted to know? The piano was right there! Eventually she sent a note home to my parents stating if they didn't get me piano lessons, she would have no choice but to flunk me.

I got piano lessons. Dad bought a baby grand; a Howard with ivory keys in walnut wood. I would escape into the music for hours. I still do.

When I turned sixteen, he asked me if I wanted a new car or a piano. Of course, it was the piano I wanted. We found a Steinway, walnut, full grand, ivory keys, and a heavenly tone. I was on track to be a concert pianist. Then, two weeks after getting my driver's license, the crash happened.

I was on my way to high school. Traffic was stopped as a tanker truck blocked the road to maneuver into the gas station. Suddenly there was an explosion of pain and sound. I had been hit from behind by a driver who was not looking and didn't see that the line of cars had stopped. This was in 1972, before cars had head rests. My neck broke. I went into shock, and then my muscles locked up and splinted. They wanted to operate and put a rod along my spine. They wanted to put my head in a halo brace and bolt it into my skull. No thank you. I went to the chiropractor every day. He kept it in place, and I used a soft collar during the day and wrapped a towel roll around it at night. I found that collar in the back of my old closet. I was really glad to see that go.

I drank rum and coke to manage the pain instead of being hooked on Darvon narcotics. I continued going to the chiropractor even in college as it slowly healed. I still go. And it did heal. I have had a career as a dancer all these years. I just retired and turned off the dance company phone this year. Oddly, I couldn't even be mad at the driver who hit me. It was my algebra teacher and I liked him. He had been distracted by another passing car of teens that had called out to him and waved hello. Life has its strange twists and turns, doesn't it? My chiropractor is now a close friend. My husband and I have gone on vacations with him, hiking in Colorado and even to Egypt. Bloom where you are planted. But I lost my perfect pitch in that crash, and I lost my ability to hold my arms up for long periods of time, which is required to practice piano. Even now, my neck is burning in pain as I write these words. The pain is ever-present. I just ignore it as best I can and keep moving forward. I never talked to my algebra teacher again. He has no idea how much that split second of inattention has taken from me and the struggles I have endured and will continue to endure for the rest of my life.

Just as well he doesn't know. It wouldn't change anything. And besides, I liked him.

The crash changed every moment of every day for the rest of my life. It dashed my dreams, but I found the grace and strength to form new ones. It could have buried me in an abyss of self-pity and hopelessness, but I chose bravery and perseverance. Bad things happen, but we always have a choice of how we will respond to them.

When you scream, I cower. When you ask, I cooperate.

Bumpy Ride—
So Many Angry Words

Did your parents ever fight? Mine did. I remember lying in that bed by the cuckoo clock with the covers pulled up over my head, gripped in fear as the angry sounds of shouting pounded in my ears. No parent ever came in to check on me. No parent ever reassured me of their love despite their own conflicts.

There were multiple times when I was buckled into the back seat of the car and a fight would break out between the two of them. My mother would actually get out of the car and walk, and my dad would drive away. I was terrified and forgotten in the back. This triggered some extreme issues of separation anxiety even into adulthood. I was afraid to love for fear of abandonment.

My husband and I worked through this. I learned to express my anxiety when it resurfaced, and he would hold me close and reassure me. Now, I need to hold and reassure that child in the back seat. It was not your fault. You did nothing to cause it, and I want to tell you that someday, when you are an adult, there will be people in your life who will love you and will not leave you. It will all turn out alright.

I always thought they would get divorced. They never did.

We moved them into an assisted living apartment a couple of weeks ago. From that big three-story house with the backyard to three rooms. Three small rooms. Dad was crying as he looked around those three rooms. "I used to have everything. Now I have nothing. My tools, my workshop, all gone."

Dad has had many strokes and uses a walker. No more big football muscles. Mom is going blind. Now they have help 24/7 and the food is good. But mostly what they still have is each other. Dad is eighty-nine, Mom is eighty-seven. Well done? Who knows? It's been a bumpy ride, but as I said, they still have each other.

> *Before you speak, let your words pass through three gates:*
> *1. Is it true?*
> *2. Is it necessary?*
> *3. Is it kind?*
>
> Sufi poet Rumi

*What do we accumulate in life
but the sum total of our relationships.*

The Wren House—
Finding New Purpose

I used to say, "My dad can fix anything."

And generally, it was true. He had a workshop in the basement, complete with a Shop Smith lathe, a large workbench, and shelves and shelves of tools. It had many piles of wood and paint cans stacked on shelves to the ceiling.

And dust—sawdust everywhere. And baby food jars and drawers full of little piles of nuts and bolts and screws and electrical parts and toilet parts and parts from old vacuum cleaners and parts from old radios and old warranty papers from who knows what, because you never knew when you might need a little piece of string. "Just as sure as you throw it out, the next day you will need it," Dad would say.

So, he never threw anything away. That has now become my job. It took two truckloads today (or by this hour, yesterday) just to clear out the garage and half of the attic. They are bringing a crew of six men and two trucks at 8:00 a.m. today. They hope they can finish. I have this overwhelming compulsion to rescue all the old stuff and pile it in my house.

When I was small, I had my own toolbox. It was an old brown wooden box with mini-sized hammer and other assorted screw drivers and such. Dad would stand me on a box at the work bench next to him and we would fix things.

We also built bird houses. Wren houses to be exact. They had tiny holes only the little songsters would fit through. We painted them sea foam green, Dad's favorite color, and would hang them in the trees in the backyard each early spring when the wrens would come shopping for a house. Each fall we would climb the ladder, take them down, and wash them out. They had their own shelf. I loved standing next to him in front of the dirty old work bench. My husband, Richard, is not too much into tools. His world is in computers; a very useful and lucrative skill to have these days. But our daughter still had the experience of standing on a chair next to Daddy. She was "little chef" and Richard was "big chef," and Saturday morning was the pancake feast. I'm glad she had that. I realize now how good that was for me. As a child it was just reality, but now in retrospect it is special. I did wish that my husband had taken more of Dad's old tools, though. Oh well. I wonder who got my old toolbox?

Be capable. Be self-reliant. Be adaptable.

Although the times I spent at the workbench were few and far between, they sent the message loud and clear: be capable. I was taught how to use the tools properly and to respect them. I learned to saw, solder, and wood burn. To paint and glue and hammer and construct. That is one area where to this day I feel capable.

Dad always said, "I can learn how to do it. Other people do this, and I'm just as smart as they are."

He would go to the library, he would ask questions of people with experience, and then he would dismantle things, build new parts for broken ones, and reassemble any number of broken appliances imaginable. He valued being self-reliant, and now so do I.

Be adaptable. Dad was always searching through his piles of wood scraps and this and that until he had created something new and wonderful.

So, my inner child always took valuable skills and lessons from that dusty workshop. It is up to me as an adult to stop and truly appreciate those examples he set. To verbalize, internalize, and be inspired by his example. Be capable. Be self-reliant. Be adaptable.

I just remembered the last year of service for the wren house. One summer we were in the yard and noticed the hole had been chewed much bigger. Dad knocked the bottom with a stick, and a little squirrel's head peeked out, his eyes blinking at the light. Adorable. But that was it for the wren house. Perhaps we should have repurposed it as a squirrel house. Finding our purpose can take some unexpected turns.

|

Is nostalgia truly a longing for the way things were, or for how we wished they were?

Coffee and Ironing— Where Do You Find Joy?

Well now it's 4 a.m. The alarm is set for 6:45 a.m. Might as well stay up and have a cup of coffee.

Mom used to drink coffee. A full pot a day, sometimes two. She had five old percolator coffee pots stuffed on the top shelf of the old pantry. They are going to Goodwill. I climbed the step ladder and hauled them down the other day. Mom says when they miss breakfast at the nursing home, the sweet girl from the kitchen brings them down a cup of coffee. They really like her. I'm glad.

I remember Mom doing piles of ironing. She taught me the proper way to iron a dress shirt. Good skill. I still use it. She would "sprinkle" the shirts with water and take a whole day to press the week's pile of Dad's dress shirts for work. Now they have steam irons. But that old  brown glass bottle with the cork topper and the tiny holes to shower the shirts was neat. I liked it. Sometimes I got to sprinkle the shirts.

As adults, we need to remember how to take joy in simplicity. The child within me was delighted to sprinkle the cute little droplets over my daddy's shirts. Just to stand on a kitchen chair next to my mommy made me feel needed and wanted. It was a simple task in a tiny kitchen, but we were together.

We need to reconnect to the truth that simply being together is joy enough.

Talk to me, my love. Let me in.

Dad's Whistle—
Can We Please Talk?

We used to play kick the can and tag in the neighborhood streets and yards until dusk. There was always someone to run with right outside the door. No matter where I was out playing, I could hear Dad whistle when it was time to come home. Even if I was upstairs in my friend's bedroom playing dolls at the other end of the street, I could hear Dad's whistle. Amazing. I always scurried home. It was nice to be called home to dinner.

That was before the kitchen remodel. It was tiny, with only just enough room for a small table. But the three of us fit just fine. I was sad when they put the TV on the end of the table. We never talked anymore over dinner. I remember it felt like a dark cloud had descended over the kitchen. I had no one to talk to except Jacques, but he was a very good listener.

Reflecting back, I think the TV was an excuse not to talk. Therefore, they didn't argue. It seemed to be a truce. Mom looked the other way when Dad left us on weekends to live a separate life.

They also put a TV at the end of the table in the assisted living apartment. When are they going to start talking again? They are about out of time. Maybe they do, just not at dinner?

Tonight, I will light two candles at my dinner table. A green one for my inner child for its healing power. A purple one for my adult self for its higher consciousness and insight. And we will talk of many things.

The language of love often uses no words.

The Playhouse—Language of Love

It's 8 a.m. and I'm back on the porch swing. Dad told me to remind the movers to empty the playhouse. It's cute that he still calls it that. My dad was never much on saying he loved me or that he was proud of me. It was always a huge surprise when someone else would tell me that Dad had been praising me and regaling them with my accomplishments. Really? I didn't think he noticed me much.

The way I gauged his affection was by the things he made for me. His dad, my grandpa "Pop," was the same way. My dad said Pop would build him cages for his pet rabbits. Come to think of it, it's strange we never had a pet rabbit when I was little. But anyway, Dad made me the playhouse. I wanted it so badly. He worked so hard on it. He leveled a spot in the yard and laid in a concrete block foundation. It was a metal garden shed with two doors that slid to the sides and three windows. I had my play table and two chairs in there, and I could go in and sit and draw, uninterrupted, all day if I liked. I know he loved me. All that time and effort for me. The language of love often uses no words.

As an adult, he made me a beautiful chimed instrument. Graduated metal bars that dangled from a lovely wooden frame and dazzled down the scale when you stroked them.

The one other gift that comes to mind is the sewing needle holder. I saw one when we were touring a historic Czech home in Spillville, Iowa, during one of our family vacations. Since Dad is Czech, I have always been proud of that heritage. Apparently, the needle holder was a Czech invention to save bits of thread and have a handy place to store your sewing needles. Since I do a lot of handwork, it had great appeal. I asked Dad to make me one, and he did! It was made of disks of six different colors of wood, stacked up in ever smaller circles with tiny holes drilled around each ring to place your needles with thread into, like a stacked-up cone. I still use it by the sewing machine regularly. The wood is all from that giant pile in the basement. You never know when you will need a tiny piece of oddly-colored wood. Now, today, that pile is going away. The moving truck is beeping its back up into the driveway. It's an odd feeling. Sorry, wood, I cannot rescue you. But I will keep using my needle holder. You will be well represented. I need to explain to the child I was that my parents had serious and complex problems in their relationship, but that was not my doing. I was the innocent caught in the crossfire.

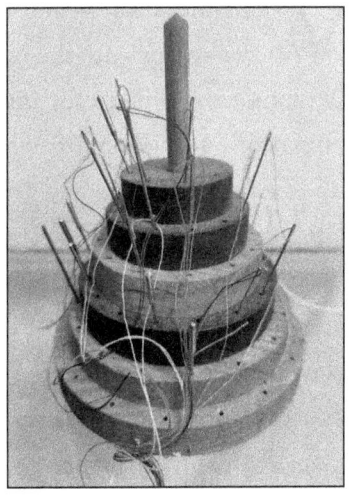

If you are the only one to remember me, it will be enough.

Trees—Rooted in My Heart

Why the sudden compulsion to write any of this down? Perhaps it's to mitigate the overwhelming sense of loss. It's late fall, or perhaps early winter for my parents. Their story is almost written. Things of our lives together here will soon be no more. They are dried up like frosted leaves and are blowing away. Soon, there will be little left but fading memories. This is my attempt to preserve a few of them.

We all have these shadows of days past. Our stories are who we are; perhaps all we are. The ancient Egyptians believed that as long as your name was remembered, you continued to live. They carved their stories in stone. We still read and remember. It's epic. In some deep place, humanity wants to be remembered.

I saw a Shirley Temple movie as a child that moved and inspired me. As she remembered things, they would appear from the past. I composed a piano/vocal song about it and performed it in the school talent show. I think I was in third grade.

There is a huge, gnarly white dogwood tree in the front yard. Dad transplanted it from the woods. Its delicate display of blooms is the backdrop of every Easter dress and bonnet photo, year after year. We grew up together. Now, its twisted limbs reach out across half the yard, stretching for the sunlight. It used to compete with several pine trees for light, making it lopsided and strange. All the pines have died; pummeled to pieces in a historic hailstorm. The dogwood survived. Seeing it now, alone, the uninformed will wonder why in the world it is so misshapen. Be careful not to judge without the rich history of the past.

I doubt it will be allowed to continue to bloom. New owners have not loved it or grown up with it, so they will not cry when it's cut down to be replaced by a more perfect, younger tree. Its leaves are turning a lovely red now. This is probably its last brilliant display. Sorry, dogwood. I cannot rescue you, but I will remember you so you will live on in an Egyptian, Shirley Temple sort of way. Bloom for me and Jacques in heaven, will you?

Like the dogwood, my childhood had its seasons of blooms and hailstorms. It left scars on my spirit. But I need to be grateful for each of their lessons. Even in adversity, we become beautiful. Damascus steel is forged of fire and folds until it becomes a thing of beauty and power.

The largest, most magnificent tree in the yard, or in the state probably, is the hackberry tree on the east side of the house. Each limb is the size of a large tree. Dad brought it in from the woods. It had a tough start. It seemed to have died. Dad had axe in hand to cut it down when he noticed that the tip of the branches had swelled. So, he waited. The rest is history. Why its roots aren't coming up through the floor of the house is a wonder. It has pushed up the sidewalk. The trunk is massive. It has an aura of power and massive strength. I can feel its life force just standing near it, and yes, I am a tree hugger, for at least this tree. It has tiny blooms in the spring, almost indistinguishable from the new leaves, but they produce berries in the fall. My parents' bedroom window looks out on it from the second story. The robins flock to it and gorge on the fermenting berries when they ripen. The effect is a circus. They get falling-over drunk. We would sit on Mom's bed and laugh. I will miss the giant hackberry with its sense of humor.

They just carried out the Christmas tree stand. So many wonderful fir trees filling the family room with the smell of fresh pine as presents piled into the room. It was hiding there under the fancy tree skirt and all of the gifts. No one saw it, but it was always there, the silent foundation for the center of every Christmas, giving sustaining water to postpone the inevitable rain of dry needles. It was the first thing to come out for the season and the last to be put away. Steadfast love does not desire recognition. Good job, old rusted tree stand. Good job, indeed. These days we set up an artificial tree with the lights already attached. Allergies, you know. I miss the pine smell. I do not miss spiky needles in the carpet, turning up randomly all year. Or maybe I do.

When I say goodbye, will it be followed by "I wish...?"

Maui—You Always Understand What I Need Most

This morning, I am on an airplane headed for LA, on a three-hour and twenty-eight-minute flight, then on to Maui, Hawaii. My wonderful husband decided I needed some beach time to reenergize and collect myself. He spoils me; it's his job, and he does it well. Thank you, darling. I started packing at 9:00 p.m. last night. I've been at the folks' house or teaching lessons all day every day with absolutely no time to plan or pack. I threw in a few things with my swimsuit. I figure I'm not going to Mars, I can buy anything there that I've forgotten.

The last time we were in Hawaii, we traveled with our daughter and my parents. We had two adjoining rooms with an ocean view. We went for Christmas and New Years. We had to pay almost double because of the holidays. What we did not know was that the trade winds shift that time of year, and it rains. We spent most of the vacation sitting in the hotel room with a deck of cards, watching CNN reports on the record-breaking storms in Maui. It rained nine inches a day for several days in a row. The roads flooded, the airport closed, and the first floor of the hotel flooded. We were counting ourselves blessed for having a second-floor room. Even the lobby flooded.

We are taking this trip in September. I pray we have preceded the shift in the trade winds. I know one thing I forgot to pack: my set of colored pencils and sketchbook. I usually carry them on every trip. You never know when the irresistible urge to draw the curves of a hibiscus flower or the exotic patterns of a fish or seashell will hit. I love seashells. They are God's ultimate artistic expression. All that fabulous beauty and color lavished in endless variety on the exoskeleton of a snail on the bottom of the ocean. Yes, you math wizards and engineers make the world modern and comfortable, but it's us artists who will have the final say. It seems that it's art and writing that has always survived through history. We judge the level of cultures of antiquity by the talent of their artisans, left behind on stone and pottery or surviving texts of literature.

I've taken up pottery. I bought a throwing wheel and am painting on stoneware. Something to leave the great-grandchildren, I guess. All the beautiful dresses with hand beading I have sewn for my daughter were for the present. Now, as I get into my last quarter of life, I've been drawn to a more lasting canvas. Drawn to . . . funny! Pardon the pun.

On our last soggy trip to Maui, we took many photos of the tropical Christmas decorations in the lobby (the day before the flood). The plan was to use them as a belated Christmas card. My husband had bought a new guy toy: a fancy little box you were supposed to download your camera memory card into to store them so you could then reuse the card. The ^%%#%& box lost all of our photos. HUGE disappointment.

To me, the annual Christmas card is a sacred ritual and historic shrine. It's a summary of the best of the year. Richard and I sit in front of the computer screen and collect the painfully selected and scrutinized photos from the travels and events of the year. Our collection of cards from years past is precious to me. I keep one from each year on my right-hand shelf by my desk, to be pulled out and leafed through periodically as the nostalgic mood hits. This year's card will have three events to immortalize. First, my perfect precious granddaughter, next our trip to Bali, and finally this impending visit to Maui. I feel so sad for my parents in their three rooms, not able to travel with us on this trip. I will be sure to share stories and photos with them upon our return. They seemed upset when we left; in a panic about saying goodbye. I kept saying, "It's only one week. The cell phone will still work. We will call you every day."

They seem to be treating each goodbye as if it may be the last, and I guess that is true. When we are young there is always tomorrow. So, sorry, Mom and Dad, I cannot rescue you, but remember that God can.

Photos for me are like portals back in time. Gazing at them, I recall in full sensory detail the experience of the original event. Losing a photo is like losing a piece of time. There are very few photos of me as a child. My parents owned a camera, but rarely used it. Film had to be developed and prints made at some expense. There is one picture of me when I was two years old: a serious round face with strawberry blonde curls and big blue eyes. It always amazes me, looking at that little face, that the child inside was often alone. I will tell her that it's all going to be alright. Someday you will take thousands of photos of the ones you love and travel the world. Be patient.

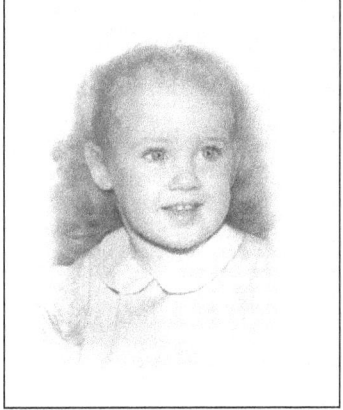

*Inspiration and hope are two sisters
with whom I wish to become friends.*

Did I Tell You About the Turtle?

Did I tell you about the turtle? My grade school mascot was a turtle. I still wonder about that—slow children seemed to be the implication. Anyway, on the last day of each school year there was an all-school picnic. We would be paraded across the street and down several blocks of the neighborhood to its end at Burnee Park. It was a small square of patchy grass with some swings and a disheveled weedy little creek running along its back border. There were always games and ice pops, but the culminating highlight event of the year was the turtle race. Poor turtles. It was the fevered goal of each of us to find a turtle before the picnic. The lucky few would proudly paint their racing number on the back of the creature's shell in the fingernail polish color of their choice. Our neighbor's dog seemed to understand our urgent need for turtles and would carry the poor, locked, closed-in-terror creatures back from the woods in its slobbery mouth to our anxiously awaiting little hands.

Well, one year, Dad brought home a poor maggot-infested turtle with a broken shell from the side of the road, obviously hit by a car and left to die. We started by giving it water from an eye dropper, and three times a day, we would soak him in a warm bath of Epsom salts.

There really were maggots eating on the poor thing's insides. The salt made them let go, and day after day, with tomatoes, lettuce, and liver pâté and continuous baths he began to heal. The legs healed and the cracks in the shell closed. He became bright-eyed and active and didn't close up when we handled him but instead came out to play. He would exercise his legs in a swimming motion as we held him afloat in the salt bath. I had the only resurrected turtle in the school race. He almost won, and would have if his sense of direction of the finish line been better. It taught me so much. Be a survivor, work through the pain, and keep your eyes on future races to be won. I drew on that turtle's will to survive and rise above being broken with insurmountable odds many times in my mind as I lay on my back, cervical towel rolled around my neck, and the pain of liquid fire running through every nerve. I figured if the turtle could survive the car crash and endure and run again, so could I.

Thank you, turtle, for your inspiration and example.

I will prove you wrong, and dance with fairies.

My First Dance Class Was Almost My Last

As a piano teacher, I aim to inspire and set a good example for my students. I hope I have touched their imagination and lit a spark within them to be creative. I have them all composing songs in their manuscript books by the second lesson.

Oddly, the teacher who inspired me the most was the one who actively tried to discourage me.

Remember that I had begged for piano lessons? Well, the same was true for dancing. But a little background first. I was born with flat feet that turned inward; pigeon-toed to the extreme. As a toddler, I could hardly balance upon those feet that got in each other's way. Mom would put special hard-soled shoes on my tiny flat feet and clamp them into a metal brace that forced them to turn out, at great distress and discomfort to me. I could not roll over or get up to go to the bathroom, I could only be trapped there on my back with pain shooting up my legs until exhaustion from crying finally gave me escape in sleep. It was tough love from my mother.

MY FIRST DANCE CLASS WAS ALMOST MY LAST

Gradually, my deformity transformed into straight, front-facing, working little feet and legs. But they were still weak, and my feet were still flat. So, when dancing was mentioned, Mom enrolled me straight away in a tap and ballet class for four-year-olds with Miss Carmen. She had been a professional ballerina, and I looked up to her as only a four-year-old could. My first class was in front of a wall of mirrors and on that shiny wooden floor. It seemed like a new magical universe. At the end of class, all the other little girls scurried off to the dressing room, giggling together in a riot of unleashed exuberance, free of the rigid discipline of the class. All but me. Miss Carmen sternly pulled Mom and me aside and motioned for us to sit down. In her forceful accent, she pointed at my feet and declared, "You know, she will never be a dancer."

Mom begged, pleading that I be allowed to continue in class. She explained it was just therapy and she had no expectations of my ever really excelling in the art of dancing. Apparently, some agreement was struck, because I was brought back by my dedicated mother week after week, then month after month, then I enrolled in jazz and caught fire. The music would drive me to ever-stronger and passionate movement until I was the best jazz dancer in the studio. At every rehearsal, I set my jaw and worked to prove Miss Carmen wrong. Never tell me I can't do a thing.

In my senior year in high school, I auditioned for a part in the cast of the Palace Show at Six Flags over Mid America. This was two years after the broken neck. There were five girls and five boys in the cast. Three of the girls from the previous year had been invited to return, leaving two open spots. My cattle call number was 2,027. I had strep throat and was taking ibuprofen and downing bags of throat lozenges.

After an all-day wait, I was finally called up. I sang a rousing "I Could Have Danced All Night," adrenaline making my strep throat a distant memory. It was perfect; the best I've ever sung. They applauded. Then they put a score of a song I had never seen in my hands and asked me to perform it. Now, all those years of piano kicked in. I could sightread and performed this new score flawlessly. They were truly amazed. They said it was a polished performance and asked me if I had ever seen the song before. I had not. Then they told me one of the judges had composed it. I said I really liked it, and that I composed music, too.

I was chosen to go into the final round of auditions: dance. All the finalists were piled in rows on stage and taught a routine. We had thirty minutes to learn it. The real problem was seeing the instructor. At each pause, I would sneak closer to the front for a better vantage point. I made the first cut. They called your name, you stepped forward, and they either said "thank you," which meant leave, or "wait for the next round."

At the end of an incredibly long day, I was one of two girls still standing on stage. I had done it. I was now a professional singer and dancer. See, Miss Carmen: never underestimate the power of the human spirit to overcome obstacles.

Which reminds me of the chair in the dance school dressing room: That first dance class, when Mom and I were finally dismissed from our lecture, I went into the now-empty dressing room in the back of the studio. It had mirrors with round light bulbs around their edges in front of little desks with tiny pink chairs in front of each one. I had never seen such a place. But it was the chair that delighted me. It was low and had gold metal hoops swirling up and overlapping to make a low back. It seemed to me that Cinderella had such a chair at the palace.

MY FIRST DANCE CLASS WAS ALMOST MY LAST

Years and years later, I enrolled my daughter in the last toddler class Miss Carmen ever taught. We were there the day she locked the studio door for the last time. We had a piece of decorated sheet cake, with "Good Luck in Your Retirement" written on it. Miss Carmen, who was never actually a "Miss" at all, but a Mrs., said that she was looking forward to playing golf with her husband. To this day, I cannot imagine her holding a golf club. But I was the very last person to walk out of the studio. I turned and asked her if I might be allowed to take one of the tiny pink chairs with the gold circle backs. She looked at me like I was crazy but said, "sure."

I just had a panic attack. That little chair was in front of my daughter's mirror in the old house. Lord, I hope the movers missed it. I'll have to run back over as soon as we get back from Maui and try to rescue it. My granddaughter needs it desperately. She just doesn't know it yet. Well, we are at 19,000 feet and in our final descent to LA. I better put the tray table in its upright position. More writing later.

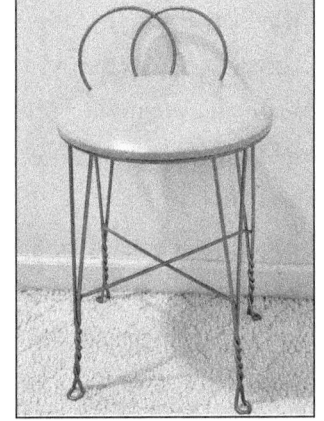

My wonderful husband had the business card of the manager of the moving company. I called while standing in line at the deli in the terminal and left a message to not take the little pink chair in my daughter's bathroom at the vanity. She called back and assured me they would not remove it and would have us do a final walk-through before they threw anything away. Big sigh. It seems that I did manage to rescue you, little Cinderella chair, at the very last second.

Some clarity, some explanation, is sometimes needed.

Timeline—So How Did That Work?

So, you are probably confused about why my daughter had a bedroom with bath at the old house. Here is a brief history in a nutshell:

I moved into the house with my parents at age two. They had the house built and are the original, and so far only, owners. I left for KU at age eighteen, after dancing my senior year and the summer at Six Flags. Breaking my dog's heart, I earned my bachelor's and master's degrees at KU in four years and married my boyfriend in my third year of college. We moved in with my folks for a short time before getting our own apartment. A couple of years later, Dad helped us buy a house about five miles west of theirs. My daughter was born. My young husband became extremely sick and sadly violent with schizophrenia. I became a single mom of a toddler alone in the new house. Mom and Dad and teenage students babysat while I taught piano lessons and built up the studio.

I joined a new church—that is yet another story—and began singing in the choir. I met my husband Richard while singing Christmas carols as duets in the church Christmas musical. The decision was made to sell my house and use those funds to put an addition onto my parents' house. So, I was back in the house I grew up in, though now it was twice as big. That way, my daughter always had a loving parent or grandparent there. I never had to worry about her being taken care of when I taught late into the evening. We lived as an extended family for thirteen years.

Then Richard and I decided we needed our own home and the freedom and privacy that it affords. My daughter was in Boston at MIT, and we bought a home a mile and a half from the folks. It was a short drive for students, and quick and easy for us to visit. There were lots of twists and turns, but time seems to unwind things into straight lines. I still think of it as my parents' house; my childhood home. We just had a long-extended visit. My house now is MY house, and we have made many changes, both large and small, to customize it to our tastes and needs.

I love my house; Richard's and my house. I plan on never ever leaving it. I want to die in my house with a contented smile. We are building chapters and chapters of memories there. But for now, I am compelled to write about times farther back and longer away.

Acceptance is neither good nor bad. Context is everything.

Liquid Soap Jars— The Grace of Acceptance

We speed up and lift off, and in seconds we are over the ocean ... hours and hours of ocean ... to find that dot of land called Maui. I love walking the streets of Lahaina, with all the cute restaurants with an ocean view and artists' boutiques. On my last trip, Mom bought a liquid soap dispenser. It was a stoneware glazed jar with a sculpted whale tail gracefully curving up the side. The glaze was in shades of deep blue to green, conjuring up images of that vast ocean. It now sits in my kitchen washed and ready for the soap or lotion of my choice. I think I will buy plumeria-scented lotion to fill it in Lahaina this trip. I moved it from beside Mom's kitchen sink before we had the movers come in for the last big push to empty it down to the walls. I rescued several other soap pump jars as well. She collected them and would change them with the cycle of seasons and holidays.

A friend of ours had her birthday on Halloween; she got the jack-o-lantern one and was thrilled. Nice. I also kept the one with the iris flowers painted on it. It has a matching bud vase and bar soap dish. I bought those for a Mother's Day gift. The guest bathroom that faces the front yard has a stained-glass window of an iris bouquet. It's lovely. So,

LIQUID SOAP JARS—THE GRACE OF ACCEPTANCE

I bought iris themed towels and accessories as gifts over the years. There was also one with a glazed decal of an elk on the front, bought on Trail Ridge Road going over the continental divide between Estes Park and Grand Lake, Colorado.

We have a friend who is a hunter. He is headed up to Montana to hunt elk this fall. I think that one has his name on it.

The soap jar with the sunflowers on it (Mom grew up in Kansas) and the ladybugs and Santa all had broken parts. They were softer ceramic. I like stoneware. It lasts.

Mom left them all behind. She is mostly blind now and can't see to fill them. She is very admirably at peace with that. It has been a slow gradual turning down of the lights and colors of the world into a dim haze at the peripheries. She just says, "Oh well, I'll use bar soap," and that is that. Amazing.

I take vision-essential vitamins to try to stave off any inherited looming threat to my vision. I paint constantly. I write daily. I read piano scores for a living. I need my eyes! I revel in colors. One of God's best gifts is the strawberry. I marvel at each one. There are more shades of red in a strawberry than anywhere else on Earth. I study in wonder after each bite, torn between looking and tasting. But in the end, they always fulfill their destiny in my tummy.

It is important never to lose your sense of wonder. Take a moment to see the exquisite beauty of the natural world around you. Keep your inner child delighted. That child within can still inform our adult selves to experience greater joy.

Slow down to notice all that your senses have to offer. The shades of red in a strawberry. The ever-changing colors of the sunrise. Close your eyes and listen to a beautiful piece of music. Let the emotions in the music flow through and into your spirit. Music communicates on a soul level. Walk into the kitchen after the quiche comes out of the oven and inhale deeply the warm, complex aromas. Your inner child can reopen realms of delight if your heart is open.

*Tragedy is often the detour to triumph.
It takes a brave soul to walk into the darkness.*

Why Belly Dance?—The Time I Almost Froze to Death

My Dad's favorite songs are "Blue Spanish Eyes" and "Red Sails in the Sunset." I learned to play them both on the piano. I don't know if Mom has any favorites. My favorites are too long to list, and cover almost every style. I guess my favorite is the one I'm listening to at that moment. I love playing Debussy on the piano. I love playing "Liebestraum" by Liszt, and I love playing Chopin and Dvorak, of course; he is family you know. For the piano, nothing beats the complexity and depth of emotion of the classical composers, but for dance it's jazz, baby, and rock, and for the past several years, Middle Eastern belly dance. No joke.

So, here's the thing. In college, I took all my PE classes in the dance studio. I had to get permission from the dean to do it. They tried to force me into sports. Not happening! I argued dance was much better exercise, and they finally relented. After graduation, I taught piano out of my living room. Once I became a single parent, I had to double my workload to keep the bank from foreclosing on the house. I interviewed at a small neighborhood dance studio which had a tiny room in the corner of the front window, with a piano stuffed in there with a large shoehorn. The bench barely fit. I taught students there and at home for several years. I worked lots of long hours. It was hard. Thank goodness I was young and strong.

The room would get so cold in the winter. There were just two walls of glass and no heat vent going into that makeshift room, so I brought in my own space heater. It was kind of nice to be back around a dance studio again. The school was tucked away in the very back side of a strip mall. The back parking lot it adjoined was behind the fire station. They would drain the hoses and wash the trucks at the top of the lot, and the water would run down the slope of the hill across the parking lot.

I taught a music pre-school class early in the morning, using one of the dance floors with an electric keyboard, long before dance classes started after school. One morning, I arrived early to set up for a little holiday party I was having for my budding young Mozarts. I had a big bag of treats and craft supplies in my arms, and was hurrying across the back parking lot to get in out of the minus zero-degree weather. In a blink, I was sprawled out on my back. I hit that frozen pavement, wrenching my left leg back into the splits in the opposite direction God had designed it to go. I sat there in shock, watching crayons roll down the frozen hill of blacktop into the sewer. That river of fire engine water had made a ribbon of black ice. There I was, unable to move, my butt freezing to the ground, and no one around. I called out for help. I screamed for help. I began to imagine the headlines, "Music teacher freezes to death, her butt frozen to pavement." I really was in serious danger of freezing to death. I was not dressed for the tundra, only for a short walk from the warm car into the warm studio. Finally, the barber across the sidewalk from the dance studio arrived to open his shop. He was an hour early. "Never get here this early," he said. "Don't know why I was compelled to get here so fast today." (Thank you, God.)

Ambulance, scans, x-rays. I needed surgery. They removed a lot of the meniscus (joint padding) in my left knee. It had broken loose and wedged itself, pinching off the circulation down to my foot. I suffered through knee surgery and was expecting to recover and be once again fully functional. But the leg just did not work, even after my knee was good. I could not lift my leg. In their rush to fix the obvious presenting problem of the knee, the hip joint was ignored. I had severed, almost completely, the nerve that goes from my torso down into my leg. I was paralyzed on my left side. This was not acceptable! I was a dancer! But every time I tried to walk, let alone dance, it would collapse under me, and I would fall. So, I did a year of physical therapy. It helped some, but I still dragged my leg forward with a limp from the hip. I could not lift it. This was just not acceptable! I began researching every dance style I could find and stumbled upon belly dance. It teaches muscle isolation and is a fluid grounded movement. I called around and enrolled in a class. It hurt; my leg would cry out and throb, no pound, in pain for a day or two after every class. But I knew from the long battle to recover from my neck injury that the pain meant it was working the muscle, and that held promise.

Well, I just fell in love with the dance, the beautiful sequined costumes, and the exotic music. I took classes for several semesters and was finally asked to join the performing company. I danced for restaurants, parties, big company events, and nursing homes. I loved it! They started sending me out to do paid gigs by myself, promising $80 or so for each show. Sometimes I was paid, but more often I was not. Oh sure, they would get it to me soon, but there was a laundry list of reasons why the check was never there. I started sending them itemized bills of shows danced and payments due. It had gotten up to $6,000 when I finally quit. I quit only their studio, not belly dance. I opened my own studio. I began teaching and booking my own shows. I got a succession of several restaurants where I would perform as house dancer. I even bought our van, in cash, with what I called "wiggle money."

Needless to say, the leg healed, the nerves grew back, and now I rarely think about that frozen fall. That dark and terrifying stumble opened a new and fulfilling career in belly dancing that I could never have imagined. Never give up, keep moving forward through the pain. Believe there are great and exciting things waiting for you on the other side. Now I can chuckle at the image of those rainbows of crayons rolling down the parking lot.

Every life has pain and purpose. Peaks and valleys. Trust that, no matter what the trauma or trial, you have within your spirit the power to endure and ultimately thrive.

So, I shared all that to say: keep dancing to the music in your life.

*Family recipes often hold the
flavor and essence of the family.*

A Bit Of History and the Ghost Who Loves Me

So now, instead of being frozen, I have a numb butt. Five hours stuffed into an airplane seat is tough . . . just saying.

My mother had me memorize English, Irish, Dutch, French, and Scotch," the nationalities of my ancestors on my mother's side. Dad was, as he liked to call it, "a pure-bred Czech. Mom was the mutt!"—wink.

We belonged to the Czech American Society and went twice a year down to the old rec hall for accordion band dance polkas and duck and goulash dinners. Ever done the duck dance? I had my first pilsner there. I knew little about Bohemia, I just knew that I loved the cheese blintzes and kolache pastries Pop would bake, and the Šunofleky (baked noodles, butter, and ham) and sauerbraten dinners and the pork with bacon dumplings. I will give you the recipes. The dumplings would sit like happy bricks in my stomach every Christmas as my aunt would turn out the wonders from her kitchen. Christmas morning was always at our house when I was little, so I did not have to leave my new toys under our tree, but in later years, my dad's younger sister picked up that baton.

I had heard a tiny bit about the migration of Dad's family. Pop came to Saint Louis in 1904 with his parents and grandparents. It was during the World's Fair, and their first impressions of the city were of awe-struck wonder. They settled in a Czech neighborhood, where most of the immigrants found no need to learn English, but continued speaking Czech.

There were still close ties to family and friends back in Prague, and eventually Pop, young then, had a marriage arranged to the eldest daughter of a general back in Prague. Then World War I started and he enlisted in the US Army.

I knew my dad's mother, my grandma, had married my grandpa "Pop" under extraordinary circumstances. Pop had been engaged to Grandma's older sister. When he came back to Prague to find her as a US soldier fighting in World War I, she was gone. Her father, my great-grandpa, had been a general in the Czech Army on the losing side. He was tortured until he went crazy and then was killed. We are not sure if they murdered the rest of the family or if they fled, but we do know that his ex-fiancée's little sister was hidden away by

the nuns. When the soldiers came looking for her, the nuns just said that she had not shown up for school. Pop found her, and took her to Saint Louis. He raised her as a little sister until she was eighteen years old and gave her the choice to stay with him as his real wife or to go. She stayed.

Grandma lost her first pregnancy. The story goes that she was just eighteen and was running and jumping over a hedge row of bushes and fell, losing the baby. She was very athletic and a gymnast at the Czech hall. They went on to have three children. The eldest daughter was named after her mother, then my dad, and then fifteen years later my dad's little sister. My dad had his father's first name and his grandpa's name for a middle name. The idea of a middle name was an American thing, as it was not done in Prague.

Grandma had sugar diabetes. Back in those days before insulin, the disease won out "early." I have little memory of her; I was a baby when she died. But I do remember feeling her hold me and love me overwhelmingly. I understand that fully now as I hold my own new granddaughter. I am sure her ghost visits me. I am most like her. She was a dancer, she loved performing in theater, and she sewed for ladies who would come to the house and commission suits, coats, and dresses. She was left-handed and would cut into mink with speed and confidence as if it were cotton; that left hand was so talented. But the nuns forced her to write with her right hand. So, she was right-handed with everything except those silver sheers. I cannot wait to be with her in heaven. We have a lot of catching up to do. I know she is going to meet me at heaven's gate. She imprinted me with her love. I remember how sweet she smelled and her kisses.

Whenever the adults in my childhood were callous or critical, I can remember back and say, "you were wrong. I am worthy of love. My grandmother loved me, and I love the little child I was."

Rejoice in every opportunity to laugh with a child.

Pop—The Grandfather who never talked to me

The grandparent that was here through my childhood was stoic Pop. We would go to his upper floor flat to visit. They owned a two-family brick house and would always have renters downstairs.

Pop did all the fixing up and maintenance on that rental, and Dad would help as he grew up. I guess buying the apartment complex was natural for Dad. That was after the lots in the woods sold, but I digress. Pop was a painter by trade, but not large brush and a roller, oh no, he hand-painted the scroll work and fanciful details along the top borders of wealthy mansions. He could paint marbling until it looked like real stone, or wood grain you had to touch to tell if it was actually wood or an image. I was told that Pop lost his lust for life when Grandma died.

I do not remember ever having a conversation with Pop. I do not remember him ever saying anything to me, except pointing to the small red velvet couch in the front room of the flat and telling me ,"Sit down."

POP—THE GRANDFATHER WHO NEVER TALKED TO ME

I did. I would sit there, alone, and stare around the room as the sounds of adult conversation came muffled from the kitchen. They would eat dinner and I would sit there hungry. I would imagine the kitchen as a grand dining hall with heaps of food on gold platters. I was only in that kitchen once, years later as a teenager. Pop was not there, having recently moved in with his oldest daughter. The kitchen was tiny and worn out. The color walked off the stained linoleum floor. A small table with two metal chairs was pushed up against the wall. There was a badly stained porcelain sink with a faucet that dripped. I remember that the dish towel stank. I was shocked and dismayed.

Why was I never allowed to join the adults? I never complained. I just sat and stared at the room. I remember how everything smelled of his cherry-scented pipe smoke. I remember a small shelf that hung on the wall near the front door. It had a miniature polka band; tiny carved wooden musicians sitting on tiny wooden beer barrels. I loved those little guys and would hear their music in my mind. I rescued that little polka band from a box in the basement. They are now playing in my curio cabinet.

Then, sometimes Pop would come in and sit in his easy chair, green I think it was, and stare out the window puffing on his pipe. He did not look at me, he just gazed out that window. Odd, he missed out on so much. I kept his old, stained pipe. It still smells like cherry wood.

Love the children in your life. They are God's greatest gift. I need to give that frightened little girl, sitting on the red velvet couch, permission to get up and move forward in life. To find her voice and be heard.

I always thought that someday, when I grew up, Pop would talk with me. As an adult, I took piano students to perform Christmas carols at his nursing home. I kept trying to get his attention until he died. I wonder if we will ever have that conversation and make up for all those lost years in the endless expanse of eternal heaven, or will he be sitting there puffing on his pipe, staring out a window?

I awoke at 2:00 a.m., my mind replaying thoughts and emotions about Pop, stuck in a loop of loss and sadness. I decided to heal and wrote him a letter. At first, I wanted to shout at him; to scold him and demand an apology. But in the end, I wrote, "I'm sorry you were broken. You missed the greatest gift the universe has to offer: the chance to laugh with your grandchild. But in a sad way, you taught me to cherish the time I have now with my own grandchildren. We both deserved better. I forgive you."

My husband and I had recently traveled to China. Now, stick with me here, you'll see how this is relevant. Our tour took us through streets and alleys lined with stalls and tables that looked to me like paper dollhouse things. Stacks of printed drawings of food, clothes, paper money, even paper houses and cars. Our guide explained they were bought by relatives for their dead. They believed a picture of a thing, when burned, would ascend in smoke to their intended and supply the item it depicts in the spirit realm. The Chinese merchants have built an entire industry around this belief.

So, I folded my letter to Pop along its long edge back and forth like a tight fan until I had a thick ribbon. Then I bent it around, end to end into a circle. Placing it in a green stoneware bowl representing Pop's chair, I set an ice cube in the center of the paper circle, representing pops frozen heart. Then I took a match and lit it. As my words turned to smoke and the ice melted, I repeated, "I forgive you."

Sometimes the goal is to quit, and that's OK.

I Quit—
And in So Doing,
I Won

Cans of green beans make great workout weights. Really, they do. My Dad was an exceptional athlete in his high school and college days. Many stories and even a few photos of him at that age, movie-star handsome and buff, still exist. He was on the swimming team and the football team. So, when I came along, he insisted I be on the swim team, too. (Thank God he didn't pick football!) But dancers are not known for their great upper body strength. As I flopped awkwardly across the pool, fighting for every breath, I hated it with passion. I had, to that date, never cut my hair. It was almost to my knees; a cascade of strawberry blonde waves that did not at all appreciate being stuffed into a swim cap, and still getting damp with chlorine. I wanted to quit. I demanded to quit. It was so BORING! Back and forth up and down the lanes one hundred times each practice. I would sing every song I could think of in my mind, but I was so BORED! It was too monotonous.

Dad and I finally struck a deal. I would quit when I won first place in a swim race. An official meet race. Okay, we had a deal. I was the absolute worst one on the team. I am sure he figured he had won that deal hands down. Now I had a goal and purpose. I began lifting green bean cans. I'd take them from the pantry and use the family room as my veggie gym. Biceps, triceps, lats, back row pulls, extensions, you name it, I tried it. And then that fateful day in the not-too-distant future finally came. My arm hit the wall and the coach pulled me out of the water in triumph and shouted in excitement "You won!" and I immediately yelled, "I quit!"

He was dumbfounded. He and Dad both argued with me. "You can't quit now, you are the most improved, you are at the top! You are the best on the team!"

Yeah, yeah, yeah, it was still the most boring thing in the world and my hair still hated the chlorine, and a deal was a deal. But I quit as a winner. Good lesson, Dad. Thanks. I was very glad to throw away those old swim caps. Seriously, Mom, why did you still have those?

Looking back, I can see that my father was trying to force his interests and passions on me to relive vicariously something he had enjoyed in his youth. Would it have been better for him to respect my choices for my own life? Of course. But I found a way to assert myself and follow my heart. Never say, "I can't." But it's perfectly acceptable to say, "I won't." Take control of your decision.

Were there people in your childhood who projected their own goals onto you?

Allow your adult self to tell the child you were that it's their right to assert their own choices. Tell your child to follow your own heart. Choose your own goals. As an exercise, I want you to fill in the blank in this sentence:

The path and passion I want to follow in my life is

_____.

Why do we value trophies?
Their plastic pillars hold up egos and praise.

Trophies—Time to Let Go

We must have thrown out fifty trophies. Oh sure, Dad and my daughter and I saved back a couple each as a memoir, but I bet we threw out another fifty.

So, do you remember Gent and Debbie were the collie children B.A.? Dad picked Gent, American Kennel Club registration "Mracek's Gentle Son" as a puppy. He recalls watching Gent's doggie mother tease her puppies with a hot dog. She had it in her mouth and was dangling it in a playful trot in front of the little ones, as they chased her around the yard, all but Gent. He sat on the side lines and watched and waited. He did not join in the game of tag. Then the moment he had been waiting for presented itself, and his mother, having forgotten about him, paused. He pounced, grabbed the prized hot dog, and ran off to eat it. Surprise attack! "That's my boy!" Dad recalls thinking.

Gent was extremely intelligent. Dad spent hours on evenings and weekends training him in obedience, hand signals, and scent discrimination; he was a champion. Gent became famous in the dog circuit. Other men would get mad and leave when Dad and Gent showed up to compete. Gent won best in show in everything he entered. When other trainers would ask for advice, Dad would say, "You have to be smarter than the dog to teach it anything." I doubt that helped his popularity.

One terrible day, Dad found Gent throwing up and sick. Someone had thrown poisoned meat over the backyard fence that poor Gent had eaten. Many vet bills later, he survived, but Gent would never again eat one bite of food that didn't come directly from Dad's hand. Dad sat on the floor with his fur son and hand-fed him for the rest of his life.

Dad built teakwood shelves across both family room walls to hold his trophies. Debbie was Gent's daughter. She had a flighty personality; she was a ditz. But when Dad got down to business, she, too, won her own share of trophies. Gent would perform on stage in plays, watching Dad's silent hand signals from the wings. They were also on TV. By the time I was old enough to remember, they had both retired from competition. But I grew up admiring the two walls of trophies, proudly displayed until today. We took photos of the trophy shelves to be sure, some with Dad standing in front of them. Their value has always been emotional. They build self-esteem and feed egos, but we can't take them with us, not even to the nursing home.

In reflection, it was never the trophies that held value. Being involved in that world, my parents would travel to shows and that created an entire social circle of friends. It seems to me that those years were the happiest for my parents, when they shared a common social circle and pursued a passion.

That observation has shaped my marriage. Richard and I share our pursuits as a team. When I wrote and illustrated my book *Friendship Flies the Sun: The Ancient Egyptian Legend of Scarab Beetle*, he did all the page layouts, typesetting, and computer work. When I was a belly dancer, he accompanied me to every show and seminar, traveling out of town for so many of them.

When I started my own dance company, he built stages and a dance studio in our house. He let me dress him in costumes and he played drums and flutes to accompany the dances.

He even became the narrator in our stage production of the book. He has done the computer work on this book. The point being, I saw from my childhood that when my parents shared activities, the marriage thrived. That inspiration has been central to our marriage. Take the positive and leave the rest.

I will protect you and nurture you till you fly away.
Then pray you will find your way home.

Big Shot and Gladis—
We Must Learn to Fly

So, we are back from Maui. It was a wonderful trip, thank you for asking. I did the final walkthrough of the house on Monday, got the dance studio chair (sigh of relief), and there were still a few things that have been overlooked. They sent a truck and two men out on Tuesday. I met them and did another walk through, pointing to this and that. The old, faded pink baby bathtub was still on a nail, hanging next to the washer and dryer. Mom used it on me, which I do not remember. But what I do remember it being used for was the duck pond.

It was when the addition on the house was completed and Richard and my daughter and I moved in, and I planted the front yard in ivy. There had always been a small lake and an empty lot behind the backyard fence. Every summer, a small flock of mallard ducks would fly in and take up residence in the lake. The pastry shop would give us their stale bread to feed the ducks. As the ivy got established, it became a thick carpet, and a duck would hide her nest in the ivy vines. Sadly, one summer the mother duck died. We never knew why, we just found her in the yard one morning with a nest full of eggs. We took the eggs inside, made a nest of cotton balls, and put a light bulb over them. We kept them moist and turned them, and one afternoon, two of them began to peck and peep, and out came the two most darling little ducklings you could ever imagine. My dad was right there, and held them and fed them, and they imprinted on him. So, he was officially a duck mother. We would grind up dry duck chow pellets into a powder and mix it with water to make por-

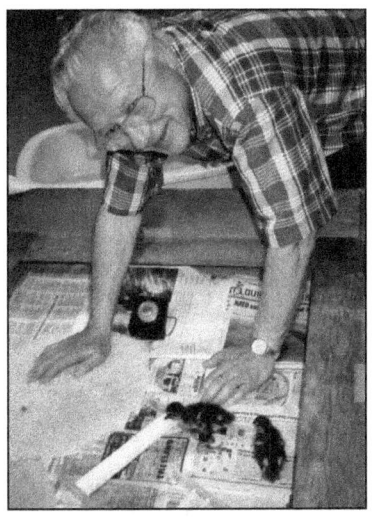

ridge. Dad split a three-inch piece of plastic tubing in half to make a feeding trough and one for drinking water.

When they were tiny, their home was just a box, but as they grew, Dad made a big wooden box about four feet square. We kept the light bulb over one corner if they wanted a warm spot, and laid down a big old towel for a cozy nest. They would climb into Dad's big palms, close their eyes, and nap, those tiny balls of fluff having baby duck dreams.

Every day, we would get down the baby bath and let them go for a swim—nice, warm, clean water to paddle around in. Dad's palms became the diving platform. They would climb up and dive in over and over. As they grew, we included field trips into the backyard. Dad would set a folding chair in the middle of the yard, and our two babies would scamper after bugs and explore. Their favorite treat was a mealworm fed to them with long tweezers. I would go on daily scavenger hunts over the yard to find cicada bug shells, and they would gobble them down like chocolate truffles. In time, we could tell one was a boy and the other a girl. My daughter's best friend named the girl Gladis, and we called the boy Big Shot.

Gladis was a cuddle baby, and wanted Dad to hold her in his lap so she could nap. Big Shot would come and lie on top of Dad's shoe, but would squirm and complain if you picked him up. Every evening, Dad would lie in the grass, and they would preen his hair with their beaks.

Dad would go in the yard and "quack," and the two would come running to him and follow him down the sidewalk through the basement door and hop back in their box to sleep at night.

We would never leave them out at night for fear of the owls and coyotes that frequented the front ivy to pounce on voles that hid beneath the dense green. Eventually, even the ducks outgrew the baby bath, and a kiddy pool was bought for the

backyard. We changed the water a couple times a week, so it was always nice and clean. They loved it! The first time it rained, they would try to peck at each drop as it hit the pool's surface.

That summer, we drove to Colorado to go hiking in the Rockies. Dad stayed home to take care of his little feathered children.

One day, Dad had them in the open field behind the back fence, and they began testing their wings. Gladis was the first to fly. She did a circle around the lake and landed back at Dad's feet. It became their daily exercise. They would fly around the lake a turn or two, land at Dad's feet, and then follow him back into the basement to their box. The flight circles got bigger and bigger, eventually even going out of sight. But they would always circle back to land at Dad's feet. Dad started walking down to the lake and encouraging them to get in. They refused. He even went into the lake himself. They would turn their noses up at the dirty water and fly back to their kiddy pool. Then, one night Gladis landed in the lake, and liked it. She quacked and quacked for Big Shot to follow. He would not leave Dad's feet. As it got dark, Dad ended up going out and calling Gladis home to the box. She followed. The next night, she again joined the flock in the lake, and called and called for Big Shot, and this time he came to her. They joined the flock. Dad was both devastated and elated. In the wild, mallards stay with their mother for ten weeks. Big Shot and Gladis stayed with Dad for ten months. They knew they had a good thing going.

I put together an album of all the Big Shot and Gladis growing up photos, and we still love the videos of them waddling in a row behind Dad, going into the basement. As parents, we strive to set a good example and raise strong, independent children,

but it still stings when they at last fly off to live their own lives. It hurts when we are no longer needed.

For three springs after, Big Shot and Gladis would fly back to our yard and lake. They would nest in our yard and proudly parade their hatchlings out for Dad to admire. They would still land at his feet. Then, one year the flock did not  return. It was so sad; we will never know why. Good thing they had their season with us several years ago. Dad can no longer walk in front to lead the way.

These ducks were a part of my daughter's childhood. I hope the patient nurturing and caring of the ducklings was a positive inspiration. The hardest thing I had to do as a parent was to put my daughter on an airplane to Boston when she left for college. I wept uncontrollably in the airport as the plane flew off. I knew she would never live at home again. She had found her wings. But the greatest blessing is the way she always circles back and includes us in her adult life. I too keep circling back. I try to help my parents when and how I can. They did their best with what they had to offer, and I can be grateful that they tried.

Indulge me, giggle with me, love the child within me.

The Christmas Tree— Making Up for Lost Time

G as used to be ten cents a gallon, and the Site Station would give a free glass tumbler or box of Kleenex with a fill-up. Around Christmastime they gave out elves. Little six-inch-tall dolls with plastic faces and red or green striped cloth bodies. I loved them. We would hide them in the dog trophies on the shelves in the family room.

The decorations were in two big boxes we stored under the stairs in the basement. It was a thrill to me when those two big boxes came out. There were strings of lights with the big bulbs that got hot and old glass  ornaments from Prague. We would wrap the front porch columns with the lights so Santa could find the house. Apparently, the lights were the original GPS. The old tree stand would come out, and we would go to the local parking lot to buy the perfect short, needled pine. Dad said the ornament hooks worked so much better on short needles. I liked it best when it was a crispy cold evening buying the tree, so they had a big fire going in the trash can and hot chocolate in Styrofoam cups. Dad would get the saw down off the work bench back wall and freshly cut the tree stalk and put it in a bucket of water until we were ready to bring the tree inside to decorate. Dad's job was always to wrap the lights round and round. As soon as I was big enough, it was my job to put on the ornaments and lastly the tinsel, thin ribbons of shiny silver metal. Each one had to be placed individually and draped just so to cover the tree from top to bottom in shimmering strands that blew when you walked by. Mom called them "ice cycles." They would reflect the colors of the lights and give the effect of a glowing magic tree. I would always save back one elf to hide in the tree. Each ornament was an old friend.

I still love my ornaments. I get one or two every vacation, and glaze and fire ceramic ornaments each year: hand-painted little angels or carousel animals or fanciful little mice.

Some years, I go into production and fire an entire kiln load of painted ornaments with each recipient's name and the year painted on the back. I made pink angel ornaments to commemorate my granddaughter's first Christmas with her name and birth date. During the final walkthrough on Tuesday, the two big Christmas boxes were still under the stairs! When I opened the lid, I was greeted with the frozen smiles of those little elves. They were in a jumbled pile, and as I drew each one out, my imagination could hear their excited chatter. I haven't seen them in so many years.

Richard and I have accumulated our own family decorations, but I will bring these little rascals into the present. It will be fun to see where my granddaughter hides them. They are in pretty good shape; nothing a little dusting and a bath can't fix. So many things are like that. Neglect hurts, but a little care can go a long way.

My mother always disliked the Christmas tree, and always took it down on December 26. I still wonder what childhood trauma made her that way. How could anyone not enjoy something so utterly beautiful and magical? I've never asked her about it, because, quite frankly, I don't want to know. I don't want any negative associations to tarnish my child's wide-eyed wonder of the Christmas tree. It's a way to stay young in spirit, to still make a special day of decorating with wine and chocolates and carols playing.

Since we have acquiesced to the "fake" tree, I no longer have a dried-up fire hazard, so I leave the tree up until Valentine's Day. The real reason I take it down then is just because I really like my Valentine's decorations, so I swap them out. Also, I realize it's a way to get back at my mother. She cannot tell me to take down my own tree in my own home. I can leave it up as long as I like. I am making up for lost time. All those days in late December and January that I still wanted my tree as a child, I'll accumulate now. I will love that little girl and indulge her. Does that make me a bit of a rebellious brat? Maybe.

*How is it you treat me with such callousness,
when all I ever wanted was your kindness.*

Augusta—
Toxic on So Many Levels

The two-girl cleaning crew arrived at 8:45 a.m. this morning. I was here to open the house for them. We did a walkthrough, and I sat on the porch swing with my writing in hand. It's now 3:45 p.m. and, except for a half hour lunch break, they have been cleaning all day. I've been here to answer the occasional question and just to keep a general eye on the progress. The back three bedrooms had hardwood floors. They were part of the original house. When my mom's dad died, we went to the little town of Augusta, Kansas, to empty his house. So really, this is my second experience emptying a house.

Augusta had an oil refinery. You could see, and smell, the dark smog that hung over the town for miles as you approached down the highway over the flat Kansas plains. We could make the drive in one long day, going past fields of sunflowers for mile after flat mile. I always begged to stop along the road so I could get out and see the sunflowers up close. They towered above my head in their glory, radar turned to track the sun. The hot, dry weeds along the field's edge always jumped with grasshoppers with each approaching step. There were windmills and oil rigs dotted here and there like aliens in the yellow flowers. But once you were in Augusta for a day or two, you no longer smelled the stink of the refinery. You would get used to it and not even notice that it was there.

Mom had left at age seventeen to go to college at Kansas University, married Dad, and moved to Saint Louis, but Granddad and Grandma stayed. So did my aunt and uncle. They all died of cancer. So did all the cousins who stayed, just saying. But when we would visit, I would sleep in my mom's old room. It was in the front of the house facing the street, but there was so little traffic that the occasional car going by really didn't keep me awake. What I loved was lying awake and listening to the train. It would clatter by and blow its whistle several times day and night, hauling crops and product for the refinery. I learned to count past one hundred with those the trains.

Granddad would take me down to the tracks in his old yellow Pontiac and stop at the crossing. We would sit together in the front seat and count the train cars as they clattered by. It was fun. I loved it. It was time alone with Granddad. We didn't have a  train by our house. I had so little affection shown to me by a grandparent growing up, so it makes me extremely aware of how important it is for me to give my time and love to my grandchildren. Those years evaporate so quickly.

In our home now, on a cloudy day with a low ceiling, you can hear the train whistle and clatter from the tracks that run through the light industrial park about five miles away to the north. I always smile when I hear that train whistle. It always transports me to Augusta.

I have nothing from Granddad. I wanted the little vanity dresser mirror from Mom's old room, but I didn't get it. I also wanted the old tin match box Granddad kept by the gas stove to light the burners. I didn't get that, either. I did have Granddad's dining room table and chairs and the beautiful matching buffet cabinet for a while. I reupholstered the seat cushions because the old red velvet was worn to the threads along the edges. I had bought an extremely expensive heavy brocade in a muted tropical pattern of leaves and flowers. It complemented the carved flourishes and lion's feet of the deep cherry wood. It was the centerpiece of the great room at my first house, and I was so proud of it. It took me back to Granddad's house, all of us sitting around the table with iced tea in the glass tumblers with Lily of the Valley printed on them, and the cicadas' loud drone just outside the back screen door and the clothesline. I remember scooting down the slanted door of the tornado shelter just to the right of the back porch and being thankful we never needed to run down its damp, spidery stairs into the darkness.

But, like my Steinway Grand piano, Mom decided she was keeping the dining room furniture when we moved into our new house. She still had her dining room set with full china cabinet, but apparently she needed two sets for all the entertaining she no longer did.

I found a walnut, bamboo-style dining table with six matching chairs and glass-top buffet table for our house instead, on page two of Craig's List. It's beautiful, fits our home perfectly, and was the exact match for my china cabinet. It was an amazing find to match a fifty-year-old china cabinet, make, and model, everything. Thank you, God. I love the new table, but that is not the point. My parents called a cousin-in-law and gave Granddad's table, chairs, and buffet to her. They really didn't want it after all. Now don't get me wrong, I'm glad it's still in the family and I am glad she likes it, but my parents managed to take my treasure from me twice, and deeply hurt me twice. It makes me wonder, was it deliberate, or are they really that ignorant of who I am and what things I hold dear? I know I shouldn't assign malice when stupidity will do. Either way it's sad.

AUGUSTA—TOXIC ON SO MANY LEVELS

Mom took up the carpet from Granddad's front room in Augusta and laid it down in the guest bedroom at her house. The junk handlers pulled it up a couple of days ago. The pad had disintegrated and left a dark brown flock stuck to the hardwood floor. The girls did their best to get it up today, but it left a stain.

It seems appropriate, in an odd way. One lifetime of memories leaves a stain on the next, and so it goes walking into the next era, generation after generation. Perhaps the new owners will sand it down and refinish it, but the easiest thing would be to lay down another rug. They would never guess the stain came from Augusta, Kansas, now would they?

I will bake a pie today and rejoice that my heart wants to.

The Apple Fridge—
And Yet it Persevered

We named our refrigerators out of necessity, really. There were three of them. The oldest was bought in 1946 and it still works today. Mom and Dad bought it for their apartment while still college students at KU. They said they had to walk it around the edges of the room to move it into the kitchen because the floors sagged in the middle so badly that they were afraid its weight might make it fall through to the first-floor apartment below. It's a white Frigidaire with a tiny box in the front center for ice; literally an ice box. It has only one door. It moved to their first house in Saint Ann, Missouri, which Dad got with a GI loan. Houses were in such short supply that he used to carry a $50 check in his pocket. Each time a house was up for sale, he would dash over to see it. Dad had just given the realtor his $50 down payment and signed the papers when two other men rushed in to buy it. I remember it just a little: the checkered linoleum kitchen floor and the shelves in my room with toys and the big box A/C in the window. The record-breaking heat one summer had my parents lying on the basement concrete floor to stay cool enough to survive, so Dad went out and spent a month's wages to buy the window unit, but back to refrigerators. That old fridge ended up in Dad's work basement with

THE APPLE FRIDGE—AND YET IT PERSEVERED

the Shop Smith lathe. We mostly kept bottles of soda pop in it, but every fall we would go to the orchard and pick our own apples. We loved Jonathan apples, which were small, red, and crispy and a bit tart. Mom would make huge pots of apple sauce on the stove and can them in jars for the next year. She used Red Hot candies in the recipe. To store all the bags of apples we would haul home, Dad made a big wooden box that fit perfectly into the 1946 fridge. Hence it became the "Apple Fridge."

When my daughter was little, I would pack a picnic of cheese and crackers, add moist washcloths to wipe off the apples, and we would drive out on the first sunny Saturday to a pick-your-own orchard. It's still Jonathan apples we like best. They make the best apple/orange pie ever. I'll give you my recipe. I made it up myself! I might have Mom's applesauce recipe you can have, too. I'll look. I rescued her card box with all her old recipes. That was a golden treasure I took home early on, but now it's buried under a pile somewhere in my house. I unpacked a big grocery bag of spice boxes from Mom's pantry into mine just this morning. One of them was apple pie spice. I think I'll make an apple pie tomorrow to celebrate the clean and empty house. I might as well celebrate. Life offers us a few big holidays to revel in, but a job well done, like emptying a three-story house bulging with fifty-six years of stuff . . . now that is an accomplishment to bake a pie for! I could be very sad, but I choose to be proud of the accomplishment, knowing I've helped my parents with a task just too big for them at this stage of life. We should all choose to celebrate whenever we can. There are certainly enough tragedies.

Anyway, the Apple Fridge was still running in an empty basement until today. We sold it to a lady who wants to put it with her vintage décor in the front of her bakery. She picked it up this afternoon. So, I suppose it's still running.

Where we choose to focus our intentions is powerful. During so many years while I was growing up, I would tell myself "that's not how to be, that's not how it should be done." I would set my intentions to be just the opposite. The apples were a delightful exception. The joy and connection to the natural world providing abundant nourishment was joy I soaked in like a sponge. It was the only time Mom preserved food in jars, and I loved it. I determined I would learn how.

On our half acre I plant with purpose. I fill my pantry with jars of pasta sauce, salsa, and jams. I also can green beans, okra, and pickles as the bounty flowers and ripens. I delight in new canning recipes. I delight in the warm earth and the wisdom of the plants to nourish and heal. There are herbs for cooking and medicine that go in the stacks of dehydrator trays.

As we reflect back on our lives, there will undoubtedly be the moments from which we can choose to be inspired. Having the discernment to focus on what you learned rather than what you lament is a matter of asking, "what gave me joy?" In all things, follow your passion. Act on the things your soul finds exciting and fulfilling; that's your higher self and your spirit guides showing you the path and the purpose for your life. When your desires are in alignment with your soul's purpose, the universe aligns to open doors of opportunities and synchronicities to smooth the path of your journey.

And so, the apple fridge perseveres as inspiration.

Hold steady and true to your own council and say no.

Melody—First There Were Many, Then One, Then None

They were all named Melody. Every doll my daughter had, and there were many, she named Melody. Often the question came at me, "Where's Melody?"

I would always be struck dumb..."ummmm"... but as time passed there was one baby doll that became her favorite, and all the other Melodies went in a box. One Halloween, when my daughter wanted to be a princess in a pink dress with the cone hat and veils hanging from its point, I sewed her and Melody matching costumes. When I sewed my daughter a heart shaped apron for Valentines Day, Melody got a matching apron, and so it went. We had a dog, but my daughter was not too interested. Her imaginary sister was Melody. When we decided to sell our house and use the proceeds to put the addition onto my folks' house, we did some cleaning out of our own. We had boxes of things stacked in the garage for Goodwill to pick up. My dad was helping me carry things out, and I saw Melody in the box. I was horrified and grabbed her out. Dad insisted my daughter had put her there, saying she was too old now for dolls and some other little girl needed her. Very much against my better judgment, I let Dad talk me into putting her back in the box.

Just as I had feared, about two days later, my daughter was hysterical. "Where is Melody!!!!!!!? How could you let her go? All these toys I care nothing about, and Melody is gone!!!!!!!"

I honestly went into trauma shock. My poor husband drove to every Goodwill store in the state looking for her. We bought another doll that looked almost alike, but I knew that would be a hollow gesture. No other doll could ever be Melody. It's kind of odd when every doll had started out being Melody. What was worse was, I had her in my hand and let someone talk me out of my better instincts. I have had that problem a lot in my life. I have let myself be pushed or bullied against my better judgment. I am finally learning to say "no" and stand my ground. It's taken the better part of sixty years. Know when to say no.

I'm standing in front of what we call the "toy closet" on the third floor. So many memories of gifts that were unwrapped at birthday parties and Christmases past. There are stacks of board games in boxes with broken lids and missing pieces. Those will go in the black yard waste bag labeled trash. But there is one box that I will place in the donate bag, because it's still like new. The replacement Melody, in her ruffled blue dress, is staring back at me through the clear plastic lid, still twisty tied to her box. She deserves to be played with, to delight a child on her own merit.

The ending of this household will for her be a new beginning. She somehow feels like a metaphor for my own inner child. Time to learn, to reset, to start over.

Gratitude is a state of being—a portal to bliss.

The Doctor's Note— I Was Finally Heard

I am still trying to empty the toy closet. It's surprising how much emotional energy seems to be stored here. In the same jumbled stack of dolls and old stuffed animals is a camel made of hand-stiched fake leather. His neck and chest are encircled with a fancy woven ribbon of orange and gold, with seven golden pom-pom tassels dangling down. He has a striped saddle of purple and pink, and long loops of gold fringe dangling around his body. His eye is drawn on with faded black marker. I bought him from a camel driver in Egypt as a souvenir from riding a great white camel. I brought him home for my daughter, but she never played with him. Turns out he is stuffed with sand, which dribbles out when he is handled. I will bring this guy back to my house to perch on top of my bookshelf. So, let me tell you the back story of riding that great white camel.

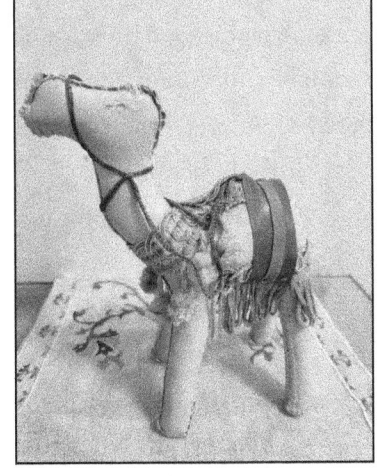

I considered myself a serious pianist from age six. In grade school, gym class was the ordeal of the day. I loved to exercise (dance), but sports were never my thing. In my first experience with volleyball, I jammed the joint of my right index finger so badly that I couldn't play the piano for weeks. I vowed never to play a sport with a ball again, and I didn't. During the doctor's visit for the finger, with x-rays, etc., I had a heart-to-heart with the doctor. To this day, I am grateful and amazed that he listened and took me seriously. Most adults laugh at young people and dismiss them. I pray I never make that mistake. This wonderful man wrote a letter to the school, explaining my serious pursuit in piano, and excused me from volleyball, basketball, and any other ball sport to protect my hands. I would be allowed to run the field instead. That letter stayed in my permanent school file for the rest of grade school, bless his heart. I know for a fact I got more actual exercise running than my classmates did standing around the court waiting for the failed attempts to serve over the net.

I wish I had a copy of that letter now. I would frame it. Now, all you sports fans, don't start writing me letters about the value of your beloved game, just understand it was not my cup of tea. I don't even remember the good doctor's name; I was so small. But what a fantastic example and impression he made on me, to always try to listen and take young ones seriously. Their lack of years does not negate the value of their thoughts.

Sadly, the jammed joint permanent damage I was trying to avoid I did to myself in later years on that same finger. About two years ago, I wanted to ride a great white camel in Egypt. They are taller than elephants and, because their knees are jointed backward, they lunge forward to stand up. The camel driver gets you up a ladder into the saddle while they are lying down. (Yes, even when they are laying down, a ladder is needed to get to the saddle.) They instruct you to lean back as far as you can, brace your legs up in the stirrups, and hold tight to the saddle horn or you will go flying headfirst over the top into the sand. I thought they were kidding, right? Wrong! The beast lunged forward with such force that my right-hand index finger jammed back over an inch into the back of my hand. This was day three of a two-week trip. I was traveling with a girlfriend and had no one to help me. I had to carry heavy luggage all over Egypt and Turkey with that broken hand. By the time I got back to the States and my chiropractor put it back in place, I had permanent joint and nerve damage. Sigh. But at least I got a good story out of it. How many people do you know who can say, "Yes, I injured my hand on a camel ride in Egypt?"

Sorry, doc.

Listen to your guides.
They will not explain but rely upon your trust.

The Robberies— Visions of the Future

I'm holding an old shoe box I pulled from the back shelf of the toy closet. Lifting the lid revealed my collection of seashells, which I had proudly displayed on the built-in shelves of my old bedroom. Holding the nautilus shell, I heard a little clunk.

I didn't see anything inside, but shaking it, there was definitely something in there. After much turning and shaking, a tiny-sized ring with a little yellow Topaz stone dropped out.

The surprise made me laugh out loud. My birthstone ring from childhood. How appropriate and poignant. A birthstone for the rebirth of my inner child. Now how did that get inside a nautilus shell, you may be wondering. Let me explain.

The paranormal has always been normal to me. Ever since the army blanket from Korea (which, come to think of it, how did I know it was Korea? As a five-year-old, I'd never even heard of the country). I have had many assorted experiences you could classify as psychic. To me, growing up, it was just how the world was. There were things your eyes saw and things your spirit saw. No big deal.

You see, I was a junior bridesmaid at my cousin's wedding, the daughter of Dad's older sister. We all went downtown to the dress shop to try on and select the bridesmaid dresses. It was all very grown up and exciting to a first grader. The night before the wedding I had a dream. I saw our house being broken into. I saw glass shatter and I saw our treasures being thrown into pillowcases. I told my parents, who totally blew me off, but I couldn't shake the images. I took all my jewelry and treasures and hid them inside the seashells on the toy shelves.

The next night it was pouring down with rain as we drove back in the dark after the reception. We were in two cars. As part of the wedding party, I had to be there extra early, so Mom took me, and Dad joined us after work. He had been out clearing trees in the woods all day. At the last traffic light before our street, two young girls were stranded in the downpour because their car had broken down. So naturally, Dad stopped to help them, and Mom drove us home.

As soon as she unlocked the kitchen door and stepped in, it was obvious that something was dreadfully wrong. All of the canisters of sugar and flour were poured out on the floor, and the drawers were pulled out and ramshackle. It took a couple of seconds of staring in the headlights to realize what had happened: we had been robbed. Mom went screaming into the house like a wild, crazy person. Instantly, it occurred to me that they might still be in the house with the robbery "in progress." I grabbed the wall phone right there at the door and called 911, reported the theft, and ran out to the edge of the driveway, prepared to run further if necessary. I kept hearing voices of assurance in my mind saying that I was safe, stay calm, and help was coming. I was as adult as I am today at that moment. When Dad finally arrived along with the police, I cried. They took everything: all the heirlooms from Prague, all of everything, except my beloved Jacques was safe, though he was traumatized and in shock, and none of my seashells had revealed their stash. They had robbed every bridesmaid at the wedding that night; an inside job from the dress shop. Never give the real wedding date, always give a fake one before, and be sure to be home on the fake date.

Regarding the broken glass I saw, it turns out that the robbers came in through the family room window in the back, and all the pillowcases were missing.

Not long after that, I had another vision, two men in ski masks coming through the ceiling of my aunt and uncle's shop. Again, I told my parents, and again I was ignored. Amazing. Guess what? Their shop was robbed by two men coming in through the ceiling vents. Two out of two.

I vowed to always listen to the warnings I seemed to be receiving. Years later, when I was newly married and in my apartment, I had another vision dream. Two men pried open the balcony sliding door of our apartment and cleaned us out. I jumped into action. We were attending an event the next night that we really couldn't get out of. So, I engraved my social security number on all the stereo components (not a good idea nowadays). I drilled holes in the sliding door track and threaded nails in and bent them around, and put a broomstick in the track. I drilled and nailed all the window latches, and then I called the police and asked for extra patrol that night due to suspicious activity. Before we left, I opened the draperies of the deck sliding door and clamped a bright work light onto a chair. I set it right in front of the door to shine out and illuminate the deck, and we left.

When we got home, there was bent metal on all the door and window frames where the crowbars had tried to force them open.

THE ROBBERIES—VISIONS OF THE FUTURE

That connection to a higher self, a higher consciousness, has always been my inner stability and companion. With no siblings, no cousins anywhere near my own age, no strong peer group of friends, and my parents passively raising me, that isolation was always tempered by my connection to the spirit realm. I was alone, but I never felt alone. There was always an inner voice of love, guidance, and comfort. I did then, and do now, believe the Great Creator (my name for God) or the Divine Universe was raising me and protecting me. The little child was lonely, but the spirit within always had a sense of belonging.

There were moments when my mature, adult voice would surface under circumstances of threat to keep me safe. And always the reassuring calm voice of a loving angel to step in and fill the void.

Every soul is here by divine love. Life, consciousness, and eternal spirit upholds all existence. We can best connect to it when our heart and mind connect in gratitude.

As a child, I would fall asleep saying, "Thank you God for Jacques."

Now the list is much longer. Allow yourself to go back to your inner child and find your own gratitude list.

*Once you have been rescued by an angel,
you will never be alone.*

My First Angel Drove Me Home

So back to grade school gym mishaps.

Ever do gymnastics? It was the one thing in gym I actually liked. I had great balance and body control from both dance and my lucky DNA. My dad's mom was a fantastic gymnast and was on the Czech society team. In later years, I had a younger first cousin who won first place in state gymnastics three times and was invited to try for the Olympic team. "But anyway . . ." as that cousin would say.

The grade school gym adjoined the lunchroom cafeteria. There were three doors that led directly between the rooms. On that fateful day in my memory, I was swinging on the parallel bars, upside down, when the bell rang, and a horde of swarming grade school boys came charging into the gym from the lunchroom. One of them crashed into the bars at full speed. As I thundered to the floor, my left knee hit the apparatus's screw and then landed in the two-inch space between the mats. I blacked out. When I woke, my knee had swollen to the size of a cantaloupe, which was impressive on that scrawny little leg.

It did not want to support my weight. Every limp tore at me in pain. Why they didn't call my mother to come and get me, I will never understand. I have, to this day, a very low opinion of school nurses just from my personal experiences; more on that later.

For some reason, I now do not remember, I had to take the late bus home. I had never done that before. Now, on every other normal day, the bus stop was at the end of my driveway. I figured I could scoot on my butt from there to the door if need be. What I didn't know was that the late bus followed a different routine. It went right past my neighborhood and stopped on the next street up, about a five-block hike to my house. I was in a panic! I tried to tell the bus driver I couldn't walk. He basically said shut up and get out. I tried to walk, to limp, I cried out, I broke out in a sweat, I looked around wildly for help, but no one was around! Now mind you, the cell phone had not yet been invented, so I was really stranded. I wondered if my parents would eventually drive the streets looking for me like a lost dog.

Then, an old blue car with a dazzling white interior pulled up, so white it shone. An absolutely lovely young lady leaned over and opened the door. "Hi, Ann, get in. I'll take you home."

Now, I knew better than to get in a strange car with a stranger. But she smiled and I felt a rush of warmth and safety and rescue flow through me, and I struggled in. We didn't say a thing to each other. She drove me straight to the end of my driveway, without me telling her directions. She knew me on a spirit level, she knew everything there was to know about me, so we sat together knowing.

I got out and shut the door, glanced at the house, and turned back to say thank you, but the car had vanished. Scoff if you want, but every word is God's truth.

As if to ice the cake, as I made it to the front door, I looked at the doorbell and wished it would ring, and it did, without my having to take the extra steps to get to it. That was fun and really cool! It was as if she was still there with me, and winking.

I believe she is still with me. Occasionally at night, and especially when I first wake up, I smell daffodils, or sometimes cinnamon. It's her, I know it is.

Soon, I guess I will never hear that doorbell ring again, pressed by a finger or by an angel. I think when I'm there by myself tomorrow, I'll just press it about twenty times in a row to memorize its classic "ding-dong."

Ditto.

The Back up Angel Found My Keys

The toy closet is one of four closets that spanned the back wall of the third floor. The linen closet is the next one to the right. Most of its contents are already gone, sent to my daughter's house or taken with my parents to their apartment.

As I lifted out two old beach towels with faded pictures of Florida, there is a story they seemed to embody.

Apparently, some of us get into more scrapes than most, and our angel needs a backup. On this occasion, I was meeting my husband for lunch. We have a revitalized neighborhood called the Delmar Loop. Once dangerous and declining, a whole new district of trendy shops with world art and incense and small ethnic restaurants lines several blocks of the main street. It became somewhat of a destination. We were frequenting the area at the time since I was the belly dancer at the Syrian restaurant on the corner. It had a glass front door with a picture of a belly dancer frosted on it and a sign that read "where garlic is king." I would dance two sets on both Friday and Saturday nights. The pay was $35, but tips ranged from good to spectacular. I changed clothes in the basement, which was down very steep, creaky, ancient wooden stairs onto a filthy concrete floor around stacks of produce crates, to a filthy old couch in the corner with a chain-pulled light bulb overhead. I would bring the two Florida beach towels to put down on the couch and the floor to have a place to sit and change. But I digress ...

So, I met Richard for lunch. The street was lined on both sides with parking meters, and at lunchtime, finding an empty space was a real challenge. Thankfully, I have always been a good parallel parker, and slid into a spot about three blocks east of the restaurant. We were going to a rather famous local restaurant, Blueberry Hill. It was where Chuck Berry had once performed on Wednesday nights. There are several rooms in the restaurant; it is like winding through an old house. Each is decorated with piles of nostalgia, and each room has a theme. We were seated in the furthest back room. We followed the hostess for what seemed like miles of twists and obstructions to our booth in the back. (You'll soon see why that detail is important.)

We were having a fun day. It was one of those bright, sunny, cool, breezy days like you see on postcards. We placed our order and were chatting when suddenly a man was standing in front of our table looking down at us. He was magnificent. Really. He was a black man with dreadlocks down to his waist in the brightest yellow and orange and red African print caftan shirt I had ever seen. He seemed to glow. We just looked up at him, blinking. He flashed a huge, bright white smile and, with a twinkle in his eyes and incredible sonorous baritone, said, looking straight at me, or through me, "Did you lose your car keys?"

I stammered, "No, I don't think so."

Then he held out my car keys in his palm and said, "Ann, you dropped your car keys."

Sure enough, there were my car keys in his hand. He placed them in my hand and turned to walk away. I quickly grabbed my wallet and pulled out a $20 bill, gave it to Richard, and said, "Give him this and thank him."

THE BACK UP ANGEL FOUND MY KEYS

Richard jumped up and ran to hand him the bill and express our appreciation, but he was gone; he had just vanished. Now, there was no way he could have done that. He would have had to walk back through the maze of winding rooms, back to the front door, and in that shirt, you could spot him a mile off. Richard even ran outside and scanned the street up and down. He had just vanished. When Richard returned, breathless, we looked at each other and realized we had been visited by an angel. I then got a flash of my car keys falling as I had put my quarter in the meter three blocks down. Someone could have picked them up and driven the car away, which would have been a financial catastrophe for us at the time. Only an angel could have known where I was, three blocks away at the very back of that restaurant, and he knew my name. And just like the beautiful lady who drove me home, he had just vanished.

Scoff if you want to, but once you have met an angel, it makes a true believer out of you. To my creator, I am still and always a child, and for that I'm grateful. The kind compassion which has held me close inspires me to extend that grace to others, and to extend that grace to myself. We are not here to be perfect; we are here to experience and learn and grow. When our inner voice chatters at us with doubts and criticisms, remember that you are so treasured that angels will come to your aid.

Fill my heart with joy, so I need look no further.

Red Flyer—A Portal

There are some toys that have become iconic in America. One of those beloved symbols is the Red Flyer wagon, with its long black stick handle folded back over its red rectangular frame. I had just such a wagon. I never really rode in it, but Scamp, Wiggle Nose, and Teddy Bear did. They were my three "stuffies" that went on adventures with Jacques and me. Scamp was a red dog with a little Scottish tam hat, Wiggle Nose was my first Easter Bunny, and teddy bear was . . . well, a teddy bear.

It seems most of us had some toys to which we attached more emotional importance than others. These three were in bed with me every night. They all were already worn and old toys when my poodle Jacques was born. I found all three in the toy chest, falling apart by now, and sadly I let them go out the door with the rubbish. I would have donated them, but honestly, they were so dirty and disintegrated that they were not fit for a new child. They were used up; they had given me their all. I was surprised at myself. It was difficult to put them in the trash. I felt guilty, like I was betraying some sacred trust, when I knew it was just worn-out cloth and sawdust. My dad's old toy monkey (appropriately named Monkey) was there too, wrapped in tissue paper. Poor Monkey actually crumbled when I picked him up. I won't tell Dad that I threw out Monkey. We'll just let that one slide.

RED FLYER—A PORTAL

I wonder why we feel the need to personify the toys. Is it a lack of enough, true human contact and interaction? Does our society isolate us in our cars and homes to the point where our children are starving for affection and a connection to the community? Sometimes, when I need comfort, I imagine my favorite toy from childhood. I imagine what that toy that loved me most would say to the child it adored.

I found the wagon in the garage, piled full of garden work gloves with the fingertips worn through and some bent and rusted trowels. It was still in pretty good shape since it had been out of the weather. I have a friend who still does a lot of gardening, so I sent it home with her in the back of her pickup truck.

Even more than when I gave the toys wagon rides, I remember my daughter's adventures in that same wagon. My husband and daughter turned it into a spaceship. They used foam sheets and cardboard to make an enclosure, complete with port-hole window. It was decorated with markers, and she would crawl inside and start the countdown. Lift off would commence with Daddy pulling her around the backyard. It was a prophecy. She now has both bachelor's and master's degrees in aerospace engineering from MIT. Cool, huh? Indulge me in a proud mother moment.

I believe it is a child's job to play, to pretend, to expand their consciousness into infinite realms of other worlds. Nothing exists until someone imagines it. Children imagine traveling to the stars and growing up to invent rockets. A vivid imagination is our greatest asset and ally. Are there things that you imagined as a child you need to bring into your reality? Can you imagine living your life in a way that you are best able to express your creativity and compassion? Until we visualize the thing, it cannot exist. Imagine yourself living your best life.

Try to understand what I do not understand.

We Hear What We Know

My dad's older sister married her high school sweetheart right after graduation. They had five children, who were all so much older than me that I called them aunts and uncles, not cousins. But when we were all still kids—they teens and me pre-school—I used to go with Mom and Dad to their hectic house, where the shouting of five children was overwhelming and intimidating. And then there were the cats. They were underfoot everywhere. The matriarch cat was mother to them all. Just a street tabby named Ambitious because she was always pregnant with litter after litter of kittens. To my tiny ears, I heard her name as "Aunt Vicious." The word "ambitious" was not in my vocabulary yet, and the underlying concept was decades out of the reach of my comprehension; and besides we were at my aunt's house, so the cat also being an aunt worked for me. I was always afraid of the vicious cat.

I used to teach piano in a room added on to the house for that express purpose. It had its own outside entrance off the back patio. No more students at the front door every half hour, parading through the middle of the house disturbing any chance of the rest of the family leading normal lives. I will miss the studio's beautiful door, all leaded glass with a beautiful, frosted pattern around the edges. It was perfect.

WE HEAR WHAT WE KNOW

Students could see me inside at the piano, and I could always see who was at the door. Every November, I would start preparing the students for our holiday recital. I would pair them up into duet teams and schedule rehearsals with the two. We would perform carols at nursing homes as our community service project. (I no longer try to teach duets; parents are too overwhelmed and overworked to bring their children to rehearsals. Sigh.)

One such instance makes me chuckle to this day. Two six-year-olds were doing quite admirably in learning "Up on the Housetop." But one of the girls would stop playing and scowl at the same place in the song every time. They were clipping along: "Up on the housetop reindeer pause," scowl. I tried to explain that in duets we don't stop because it messes up our partner, but every time in the same place, she would stop and scowl. Finally, I asked, "Why do you stop there? What is wrong?"

Her aggravated response was, "Because everyone knows reindeer do not have paws, they have hooves!"

Then, just tonight, in a lesson with a young girl whose family moved here from Russia, we were playing a cowboy song. The words were, "say hello to prairie dogs." Her eyes got big, and she asked, "Do dogs fold their paws and pray in America?"

She heard "praying dogs." It took some explaining.

So, the point being, sometimes we hear what we know, not what is being said. It is up to the speaker to be sure that the statement is understood. So many times, angry words or deeds could be smoothed over and differences bridged if we really try to hear and understand what is being said. We need to listen better.

We cannot grow roots without fertile soil. What lies below the surface dictates our destiny.

The Garden—
It's Not What You Think

Living in an urban environment, I was afraid my daughter would think our vegetables just appeared on the shelves at the grocer, so I decided to plant a garden. I dug up a smallish rectangle of sod near the locale of the doghouse in the backyard and got some seeds. Carrots, Brussels sprouts, and snow peas are the ones I remember. I made sure that she helped at each stage of digging and planting and watering. All I can say is that it's a good thing we were not trying to live off of those efforts. By fall, the Brussels sprouts were still the size of peas. We ended up harvesting the tiniest sprouts you ever saw. We imagined we were tiny fairies having a feast. I had soaked them in sugar water overnight to be sure she liked them.

The snow peas did quite well, and we ate several right off the vine, until the Saint Louis heat set in and they withered.

The carrots, though . . . we thought we had the biggest, best carrots in the world. As we watered and waited, they got big leafy plumbs and the orange tops got bigger and bigger around. They got almost four inches at the top, and we decided it was time to harvest. We were so excited, expecting to pull up a carrot big enough to feed the whole family. To our shock and amazement, when we pulled it up, it looked like an orange pancake. It was four inches around and about a half-inch long. We burst into laughter! Apparently, our Missouri clay was so hard that the poor thing couldn't grow down, so it grew out the sides. It just proves the old adage, "Don't count your chickens before they hatch." Or, in the case of our family, "Don't plan the meal until you pull the carrot." It still has truth. So often, what we see on the surface is not a true reflection of what is underneath. Sometimes we need to do a little digging to get to the truth.

Imagine with me, in endless flights of fantasy.

Cloud Spaceships and Betrayal

There is a pile of rusted shovels and broken rakes in the garage that I need to haul out. Leaning up against them were two wheels with metal brackets and rusted bolts. At first, I couldn't think what in the world they were. Then I smiled when I realized that they were training wheels.

I used to love to ride my bicycle around the neighborhood. I never went anywhere, just up the hill and around the bend and back to our house. My bike was purple, of course, and I started with Dad running alongside and those training wheels flanking the back wheel. Riding gave me a sense of imagined freedom. Being alone most of the time, I invented games to play in my head. I'd imagine riding to China or, better yet, to another galaxy. On bright summer days with big puffy clouds, I'd imagine the shifting shadows the clouds cast were actually made by an alien spacecraft, and I would have to outrun them or dodge between them like a *Star Wars* fighter.

Remember, my dad was an aerospace engineer and an inventor. We always had models of Mars landing vehicles being constructed on his workbench or drawings of some fantastic space idea on his drafting board. My dad invented the heat shield for the bottom of the Gemini space capsule and the wing folding mechanism for the Space Shuttle. He has two Mars landing models in his apartment right now. So, a bike being a spacecraft was natural for me. It was just a game to play pretend and have some fun.

One summer, a family moved in three doors down and had a daughter roughly my age. Sometimes she would be out riding on her bike too, and we would ride together. I asked her if she wanted to play spaceship and explained the riding game. She said she didn't and left. Well, okay then. I didn't think anything of it. A couple days later when I saw her outside, she told me her mom said she couldn't play with me anymore. "Why?" I asked.

"Because I told her you think cloud shadows are spaceships, and Mom says you are crazy, and I can't play with you," she said in a flat, blunt tone.

"It's just a pretend game. Don't you ever play pretend?" I asked, my eyes wide in disbelief.

"No, and you are crazy," she snapped and turned and rode off.

I never played with her again, and that was okay with me. Anyone with no imagination wouldn't be any fun to play with, anyway. The ripple effect of it was she started telling all the "kick the can" players of the neighborhood that her mother said I was crazy, and that no one should play with me. I spent the rest of that summer inside sewing doll clothes. I taught myself how to make patterns that would fit the dolls and I made myself a doll house out of a box. I even painted the walls of the rooms and decorated them. I inherited my grandma's talent for sewing. I had a lovely summer.

I am comforted in the knowing that the isolation of that summer taught me to be self-sufficient and creative. I never played outside in the neighborhood again. The friends I thought I had turned on me like vipers. They had played with me and known me for years, and yet one newcomer with an evil heart was all it took for them to shun me. Why didn't they stand up for me? Why didn't they look to their own experience? And yet, I have drawn on the ability to create my own joy all my life. I will tell my child within: you are enough.

I reflect now on how stupid that mother was. I bet she forced that girl to color inside the lines of the coloring books, too. What a perfect upbringing for a robot. I hated coloring books. Oh, I loved to color; the more color choices, the better, but give me a blank sheet of paper. I always wanted to make my own lines. I still get excited when I see a sale on blank canvases at the art store. Give me a blank sheet of paper and I am entertained for hours . . . like now, for example. It's midnight and I just remembered this story, so I had to get up and find a sheet of paper to write it down.

Even as a child, I was somehow aware that this summer of solitude was a blessing. It taught me to go within; to tap into the creative flow of the universe to the blissful realm of imagination. I taught myself to design and sew patterns that fit those tiny dolls that were my willing companions, a skill I drew on heavily decades later for my dance company. I am thankful now for the opportunity to revisit those days in the basement at the sewing machine. I learned that I was enough. Everything I needed was already within me. I experienced such creative flow that time disappeared and joy was abundant. That same space of creative energy is still my bliss, whether I'm writing, painting, or composing. It is good to step back and appreciate those formative experiences in childhood that gifted us strengths and talents. What seemed cruel at first glance was a necessary lesson for the adult I was to become.

I will tell my child within: you are enough.

We should always be healing, since there seems to always be something from which we need to heal.

The Scar—Even This Can Heal

So, speaking of bicycles, I outgrew mine. It got to where my knees were getting ever closer to the handlebars. One crisp spring day, I got the bike out from its winter sleep in the garage for a spin up the hill and back. It was more difficult than I remembered to pedal. My legs just did not want to be stuffed between the seat and the handles. With great determination, I tried to go fast on the downhill home stretch. Big mistake. There was a screw in the handlebar, whose jagged point stuck down just past the surface under the bar. As my knee hit the underside of the handlebar, that point of the screw jabbed into the back of my knee and ripped my leg open all the way up to my hip as I pedaled. I had split my leg open knee to hip in a jagged line about a half inch deep. I fell off the bike and screamed.

Luckily, Mom and Dad were both home and I was rushed to the doctor. But I had an ugly red scar the length of my right leg for years. It eventually turned white, and then got thinner and shorter until now it's completely gone without a trace.

Sometimes there are snares and dangers lurking we just do not know about. If I had better sense, I would have realized the bike was just too small and not gotten on, but my memory of how things used to be overruled my perception of current reality.

It's sort of like aging. In my mind, I still see myself as the professional dancer in the tiny, toned body, but my mirror does not agree.

But we have a way of healing and adapting. As I mentioned, I retired from dancing and turned off the dance company phone. That really hurt and opened a wound. But I realize no one wants to see a sixty-year-old belly dancer, no matter how well I still dance. And as I move on to other creative endeavors, that scar will fade too, until there is no trace of it left.

The important thing is to keep reinventing yourself. It is never too late to imagine the next adventure or the next creative project. The vacuum closing the dance company created filled so fast and so completely that now I can't imagine how I ever had time to do it at all. Embrace the flow of change and evolve.

*We are beings of light, experiencing a body.
It's all a matter of energetics and perspective.*

Auras I Massaged

Remember the shoebox of seashells? There was a penny in the bottom of the box. As I placed my shells onto their new home on a shelf in my house, I picked up the penny to toss it into my coin purse. It flipped over to reveal a transparent coating of red glass. It had been copper enameled. The penny went into my jewelry box for safekeeping instead.

As a child, I finally made a friend who would invite me over to play. She had a tiny copper enamel kiln, and her mom would give us pennies to melt powdered glass onto. I wonder if she is still alive.

That reminds me of another bicycle accident that saved my friend's life. When I was in fourth grade, I made a friend at school. She was in my class, and we were great friends. I had very few of those, so she was extra special to me. She would invite me over to her house to play after school.

Her family was Irish. They were Catholic and had a huge family. To this day, I don't know how many kids were in the family; they seemed to be everywhere at once. but I think my friend was the third from the youngest. Her dad worked from home. I don't know what he did for his job, but I would be fascinated seeing him move through the house. He had both legs amputated from cancer.

They lived in the big old farmhouse at the end of the street: a two-story white frame house with creaky floors that slanted down between rooms. The entire neighborhood had been in their front yard at one time. They had sold the land to a developer, who put lots around a U-shaped drive with a green space common ground in the middle. There was a grove of native Missouri persimmon trees on the common ground toward the front left side, and every fall we would pick buckets of the ripe orange fruit. The darling little balls would litter the ground under the trees. It wasn't ready until it was a gooey paste, sweet as candy, usually after the first frost. Her mom would bake persimmon puddings, which were like pumpkin pie without a crust, and a richer, warmer flavor that always made me imagine deer and raccoons feasting on them at night.

They had an old tire hung from a rope in the backyard we could sit in and spin. It dangled from an ancient maple tree, and when the seeds would whirly bird down spinning, we would try to catch them as we swung around.

We both liked to ride bikes around the neighborhood. There was always an extra bike for me to jump on and join in the racing up and down the pavement. We would jump the curbs and try to do wheelie pop ups, until she fell off the bike and hit her leg hard on the curb. It bruised black and hurt a lot, and it just didn't heal. A week later it was worse. We all got worried. Many doctors later, she was diagnosed with cancer. The bike accident had caught it in time, they hoped. But my friend had her left leg and lung amputated. It was brutal.

In the many long weeks of convalescence, I would go over to her house to sit at her bedside and visit. We would talk and I would get her drinks of water and hold her hand. But the one thing I did for her that she said no one else would do was massage her leg. Her missing leg. She said she could feel my soothing touch and it took the pain away. I would see her missing leg in my mind and rub and massage the air where it should have been. She would stop crying and relax and eventually fall asleep, and I would tip-toe out and go home.

They moved to another state not long after. We were too young to really write letters, and there was no internet yet, and long-distance phone calls were very expensive. She came back one time to visit with a prosthetic leg. It looked huge and fat in comparison to her skinny other leg. I could tell it hurt her.

This experience solidified my belief that we are all spirits that inhabit a body. If the body suddenly changes, the spirit does not necessarily change with it. Her life force or aura still believed her leg was there. No one else believed her when she said she felt the missing leg. I would ask her where her leg was before sitting on the bed, because if I sat on it, she would scream out in pain.

I still go to the neighborhood common ground and pick up buckets of persimmons. I bake persimmon puddings. I have both the original recipe and my own healthier version. I'll share them with you. Once, a friend of mine went to fill a bucket for me, and the elderly neighbor came out of her house and said, "Those persimmons are always picked by a red headed lady."

My friend explained that he was, in fact, gathering them for me. "Well, all right then. She has been picking them for all these years."

Yes, I have, and I always remember the lovely Irish girl with the blonde hair, blue eyes, and the aura that I massaged.

She was my one true friend. I didn't make another until high school. I felt abandoned when she moved away. I can now take comfort in knowing I was the one unique being who could help her through her horrible ordeal. I was the friend she needed. So rather than thinking of my loss, I will focus on her gain.

My ordinary life is extraordinary when you enter the room.

Oatmeal—Life Needs Spice

I made breakfast this morning in my mom's old copper bottom pot. I seem to have lost the lid in the move, but I didn't need it anyway. I remembered that I had a box of steel cut Irish oats in the pantry. Remembering my Irish grade school friend made me think of them. With fall upon us, I'm reaching for my fluffy lavender robe in the morning to keep the shivers away. Oatmeal sounded good for the first time of the season. I asked my husband if oatmeal was okay for breakfast, and he replied, "If you have things to add to it. Didn't you give the folks our cinnamon?"

Well, yes, I had, but I found another, and it got me thinking. While oats are the foundation and keep us alive, it's often the little extras we bring to life that make it enjoyable. To my two cups of oats, I added four cups of water, a carton of plain Greek yogurt and a half cup of raisins. I served it with raw honey drizzled on top and, of course, cinnamon. Like I tell my music students, the dissonance is like cinnamon. Composers use those intervals like spice to add emotional depth to the music. You wouldn't want an entire symphony of clashing sevenths, but then you wouldn't sit down to eat a bowl of cinnamon, either.

I try to look at life's obstacles and problems like that. No one wants every day to be filled with stomach flu or flat tires, but when we do have challenges and obstacles sprinkled in, it makes us stronger and more interesting. As we look back over life, the obstacles we have overcome should make us better people. They are often our best stories.

I had to stand over the stove and stir the pot for several minutes this morning. But when we stir the pot and take the heat, something wonderful can result.

Children do not have the perspective to look back over time. They see only the present situation as if it were the entirety of reality. I will tell my inner child: this is just a puzzle piece. You will see how it fits into the whole. It will interlock with so many other experiences to create a vast and beautiful picture of who you will become.

Never relinquish your power. It is your responsibility and privilege to be your own advocate.

The Pine Tree That Nearly Killed My Father

Everything takes longer than you think it will. I gave the movers a key to the house so they could come in on Sunday while we were in Maui to finish hauling out the basement. It took another truck. And even after I got back, there were still things left. The guys had to get a ladder and cut down the strings from the pulleys that Dad had tied to the ceiling joist to exercise and rehab. So, here's what happened:

There was a giant white pine planted in the front of the house by my parents' bedroom windows. The folks' room had two walls of windows, making the corner: one facing south and front, the other east on the side by the hackberry tree.

Dad decided that some of the lower pine limbs were just too big and needed to be pruned. He got the extension ladder and propped it on one of those heavy limbs and began to saw away at it. When he cut through and the limb fell to the ground, it sprung up violently with the sudden release of the weight, throwing the ladder backward with Dad still on top. He fell backward over fifteen feet, hitting flat on his back in the ivy. His head missed the terracotta sewer pipe that stuck up out of the ground by a mere half-inch; a half-inch to the left and he would have been killed. As it was, the wind was knocked out of him, to say the least. The entire back of his body, head to toe, turned black as the bruises surfaced. He had also broken his shoulder bone. We found him sitting on the porch swing dazed. He just said he thought he might be hurt. He was in shock, I think. The doctor recommended that he do weight pull downs to rehab. So Dad, being an overachiever, set up the pulleys from the basement rafters and worked on them a couple of times a day. It was the worst possible advice he could have been given. The strain made the bone separate and it would not heal. To this day, the bone is in two pieces. You immobilize a broken bone, not exercise it. But Dad blindly followed the doctor's advice because he was the doctor. Now, not that I have anything at all against doctors, but we need to remember that they are people first, and people make mistakes. Always get another opinion when the alarm bells go off in your head with, "That doesn't make sense." Then get a third opinion, then a fourth. Do your own research, be your own health advocate. Take responsibility for your own health and wellbeing.

As a joke, we answered the phone for a while with, "Dad's tree trimming service."

It seems that the past few winters have gotten colder, and the ice storms more severe in Saint Louis. We were all grateful to be in our warm beds one night as the ice storm howled outside the windows. Then, suddenly, we heard a huge thud of something crashing on the roof. It came from the direction of my parents' room. As we bolted up to find slippers and robes, there was another thud, and then another as we rushed down the hall. Then another, and another. The folks were safe, but something was landing on the roof above their bedroom with alarming force. We opened the draperies and tried to peer out into the storm. Between the dark and the ice coming down, we couldn't see a thing. The thuds kept coming for a long time, then stopped. Nothing had come through the roof, but we were anxious to inspect the roof at first light. In the morning, we discovered the world's largest toothpick standing just outside the folk's bedroom. The giant white pine, which had stood at least another story above the house, shading the front of the house on that east end, had been stripped of every branch. The weight of the ice had broken off every limb, one by one, from the smallest at the top, all the way down the trunk. The limbs that hung over the house had hit the roof on their way down. What was left was the giant trunk, every limb snapped off at its base. Too bad Dad had tried to cut limbs himself a few years earlier. If we had only known. We had the trunk cut down. This time, Dad called a real tree service. It left a large flat stump. I sat a concrete statue of Quan Yin on it. Eventually, the ivy grew over it until now it's completely hidden. The new owners will never know about the giant white pine that almost killed my father.

I suspect our tendency to blindly obey an authority figure, such as a doctor, stems from our childhood. The more tightly controlled and repressed we grew up, the more we give up our own power. To think through situations in a creative, empowered way also requires a willingness to assume the responsibility for our actions. Whenever I hear the limiting voices from childhood telling me to passively obey, I take several deep breaths. Then I tell my inner child: you can choose your own path. Be strong. Be courageous.

I do not have to see you to know you are there.

The Green Cake—
My Inspiration

I have a friend who I love. We don't see each other very often and we email in spurts, but her place in my inner circle is permanent. Her mom and mine were best friends. Our parents met as members of the collie club, and her parents had the litter of puppies my dad got his best friend Gent from.

My mom tells this story about when we were born. Both women were expectant mothers together. Christie was born two weeks before me, and her mother called mine from the recovery room, saying, "It's awful, don't do it!" as my mom was huge and due any day!

So, I have known Christie all my life. I played down the street at her house for years. Her mother was wonderful to me, and to this day I find myself imitating her as the highest form of compliment. When my parents went on vacation, I stayed with them.

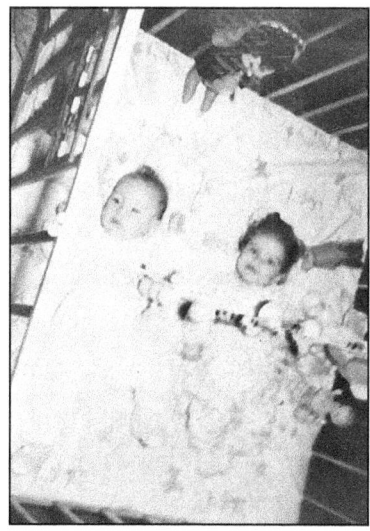

Christie has always been an artist. She paints. I remember her second birthday party as one of my first clear memories. We were in her backyard. There was a small round, above-ground swimming pool on one side, and a picnic table set up. The grass was mostly trampled by kids and her three big dogs, collies, of course, and a lovable mutt.

I vaguely remember a magic show, but what impressed and astonished me most was the birthday cake her mom had baked. It was bright green inside! That has always been Christie, full of fun and the unexpected.

We spent hours playing with plastic horses. She was horse crazy, as I called it. I didn't much care for them, but I wanted to be with Christie, and that was what she wanted to do. (As an adult, she bought her daughter her own real horse.)

Their house was inspiring, and I fit in there. Her mom was Italian; she talked loudly and said "shit" every other word. She never meant any harm by it, it was just a habit, and her eyes would twinkle. She grew her own herbs along the fence line in the backyard and cooked like a chef. She made two dinners every day of her married life. Her husband would only eat a baked potato and a pork chop for dinner. Every night it was the same. (I will say one thing positive for her husband, though: he played the piano!) So, she would make his meal, and then something wonderful for the rest of us. She would say she wanted us to grow up loving all kinds of foods, and we did. Now, I grow my own herbs and veggies in garden barrels on my deck so I can step out from the kitchen for fresh ingredients all summer and into the fall.

Best of all, she knew how to sew. She made Christie's clothes and her little sister's when she came along, as well. I was so drawn to her for that. I guess because of my grandma. One year she made all of us sock monkey dolls. I have a soft spot for those dolls to this day. (I bought Christie and I both sock monkey Christmas ornaments as a reminder of those long ago days.) I took sewing lessons for three summers in the basement of a lady who would take in four or five girls at a time to teach. I loved sewing so much! I still do.

Because both of our parents moved away from their first little house, we saw each other less and less. We never went to the same school. I would have liked to have spent more time with her. When she got married, they moved to California, and later to Chicago. She was the bridesmaid for my first wedding. My daughter was about three when her daughter was born. I had many baby shower gifts for Christie, but I also bought lots of fabric and patterns for baby clothes as a gift for her mother, the grandma-to-be. She loved it, and said, "That was the neatest thing you could have done!"

I was so glad. Both of her parents are gone now. I didn't know about her mom's funeral. That really hurt. I got a call from my aunt who just happened to see the notice in the paper about her dad's funeral and Richard and I went. I wish so much she would have called me and let me know.

We have visited off and on. Richard and I drove to Chicago for visits, more so when our children were small. She is a gifted artist. Her painting style had moved from Impressionist to modern to abstract, but was always a flamboyant expression of her free spirit. I consider myself her biggest fan. She used her entire house as a canvas. Every wall and closet door were covered in collage and painted fantasy worlds.

When the kids grew up and moved out, she sold the house and moved downtown to a high-rise apartment with a lake view on one side and city view on the other. (I always wondered who bought all those painted walls.) The new apartment is impressive. When she had the house and yard in the "burbs," she had a pack of tiny yorkies that would run through the rooms in a whirlwind of excited yaps. Now on the twenty-fifth floor, she has two huge bull dogs that she must go down the freight elevator with to walk several times a day. It seems kind of backward to me, but she grew up with big dogs and I guess they fill the empty nest.

Christie used to say that someday, when we were both old and widowed, we would live together in that big house. We would turn the third floor into our painting studio and keep each other company. I would have liked that, but sadly that house will be gone soon. Maybe, if ever we are both old and lonely, we can find a space where we can paint side by side.

It would have been easy to drift away completely from this friendship, but my inner child clings on. I find strength and comfort in knowing there is one friend I have always known.

We were texting yesterday, and I mentioned I get up at 3:00 a.m. to write this book. She said she gets up at 3:00 a.m. every morning to paint and frame art in her studio. We are creative souls drawing parallel lines. I believe it is important to build your tribe. Cultivate meaningful relationships with like-minded souls. It only takes a few. I will hold my inner child close and tell her: someday, you will have a circle of support.

I take a deep breath in gratitude, place my fingers on the piano keys, and the music begins to flow. I hear each note as an empathic download.

Pianos—The Focal Point of My Existence

Tonight, I cried. I cried as I relived a great loss, and I cried for sheer beauty. It took me completely by surprise. I was shocked and unprepared. As I sobbed, I struggled to be silent as waves of memory and emotion flooded over me. Every note memorized, my fingers moving involuntarily with every note, every breath synchronized with each downbeat.

I was given two free tickets to tonight's symphony from the local Steinway piano store, where we bought my newest Steinway piano and where I hold my annual June recital for students. The tickets arrived in the mail, and without even a glance, I hurriedly stuffed them in the checkbook so I wouldn't lose them. We were at the Apple Butter Festival in Kimmswick, Missouri, all day, and then hurried to get changed and out the door to the concert. The first number was Beethoven's Egmont Overture; very enjoyable. The piano soloist took the stage to applause, and then the opening of "my" concerto—Schumann Piano Concerto in A minor Op. 54—began to play. It was like being instantly transported back in time. That was my concerto. I started learning it when I was fourteen years old. I spent hours practicing every day for about twenty months until I could perform it in its entirety, concert-ready, from memory. My teacher was trying to find a symphony that would listen to my performance. Then, two weeks after my sixteenth birthday, my neck was broken in the crash. I never had the opportunity to perform it. And until tonight, I have never listened to the Schumann piano concerto again. It was just too painful. I never expected to hear it again. I have been deliberately avoiding it. I feel like tonight 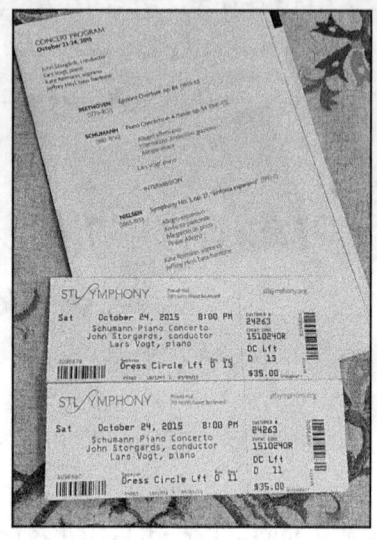 was an ambush. God forced me to hear it again to grieve and cry. I have blocked this pain for decades, but somehow now, as I let go of so much, it seems that the right time has come to also let go of this inner suffering. If I had been able to fulfill my career goal as a concert pianist, I would have traveled, lived out of a suitcase, and traded my family for endless hours of practice. Perhaps that was never the solitary life God had wanted for me. Perhaps I was so stubborn in my pursuit that it took a trauma so huge that it almost killed me to force me to change paths.

When I was in college, I spent almost every dime I had made singing and dancing in the Palace Show at Six Flags on a Baldwin upright piano. All the other cast members were buying clothes and other luxuries, and they kept teasing me about saving my money. I bought myself a silver and turquoise bracelet to have a nice keepsake to remember the experience by, but then every paycheck went into the savings account. I just knew I would need it later. The piano was my "later." (As an aside, years later my dad took that bracelet out of my jewelry box and gave it to my daughter without telling me. I can't imagine why; it wasn't his to give. I took it back and explained the situation to her. She knows I will give it to her in the future. It is mine to give, not his.)

I had the piano in my dorm room to facilitate six hours or so a day of homework that required a piano. This was 1975, and keyboards had not been invented yet. As a music composition major, I took an electronic music class. The electronic music studio was housed behind lock and key in a room about the size of a large walk-in closet. It had the mystique of a secret weapons facility. Each "sound" was produced from a rectangular metal box about ten inches by five inches that we would patch cord together like old time telephone operators. We could connect boxes that would produce different sound waves, like sine wave or saw tooth, or white noise or pink noise. Every note needed binary code written for the attack, sustain, and release. I decided it was years away from being anything useful and only took one class.

The fifth floor of the music building had tiny rooms with a piano in each. You could sign up for practice times, but it started with PhDs, then grads, then seniors, and by the time it got down to freshman there were no times left to reserve. So, the piano in my dorm room was my only viable option. Tease me for saving if you want to, but I paid cash for the Baldwin upright.

I draped sheets of felt over a dowel rod and hung them inside the piano in front of the strings to mute it, so it was barely audible to me as I worked. The stereos blasting in all the other rooms were much louder. The bench pushed up against the bed, and I would walk on top of the bench to get to my desk. Since there was no room for a chair, I sat on the end of the piano bench at the desk. The quarters were tight. Thankfully, I had a private room, or I guess I would have been sleeping under the bench.

Later, living with the folks, I was teaching on the Baldwin upright piano, and recording students on the Howard baby grand in the room added onto the house for that purpose, but my piano, my sixteenth birthday present Steinway, was upstairs in the living room for my private use; no kids would be banging on it or scratching their shoe buckles across the bench. My husband and I moved into our current house five and a half years ago, and I, of course, bought a house that had a great room that would fit all three pianos. My mother refused to let me move the Steinway to my new home. She didn't want the living room to look empty. She had never played a note on it in her life, and it wasn't hers to begin with. I hated her for it; truly hated her. I saw that shallow selfish act as a deliberate way to axe out part of my soul. But rather than start World War III, my husband bought me a new Steinway grand in gorgeous Missouri walnut. We are still making payments on it. Now, with the dismantling of the folks' house, my Steinway piano needed to go. I gave my daughter the Howard baby grand, and, at long last, moved my first Steinway, my sixteenth birthday Steinway, into my music studio at our house.

So, what did my mother accomplish? She put a permanent wall up between us. She proved she does not understand or care to understand my spirit. I have forgiven her, but I cannot forget.

I glanced in the mirror tonight at the symphony. I don't recognize that old woman. Tonight, I was fifteen and playing every note with Lars Voft. He did a fabulous job, bravo, and I should know. Maybe now at last I can start to enjoy the piano concerto again, and to enjoy my first Steinway, and let the tears wash away so much anger and pain I have been holding on to. There is a time for being tough, but there is also a time for tears.

As adults, our society demands that we hide our emotions, but repressed grief is destructive. Find a safe place and let go, let the tears flow. Give the child within permission to grieve the losses and hurt. Flowing water is very magically healing for this. A stream in the forest, a lake in a park, or even letting a warm shower flow over you. Into a pot of water, place a sprig of rosemary and a cinnamon stick for their protection and healing. Then, float rose petals on top. Bring it to a boil, then let it simmer. Breathe in its steam, then strain and drink the tea. Tell your inner child they are safe, healing, and loved.

Open your eyes to nature's abundant gifts.
Sweat equity and vision are all she requires.

Daylilies—
Abundance and Resilience

Winter is coming. We had a hard freeze last night, and it got down to twenty-one degrees. I hope we transplanted the toad lilies soon enough for them to survive. The name sounds ugly, but in fact they have exotic purple blooms that resemble spotted orchids. I had a large clump of them in the backyard at the folks' house, and since they bloom in October, I was able to spot them. Richard dug them up and planted them under our maple tree by the back patio. I should have tried to transplant some of the daylilies, but really our new yard doesn't have a great spot for them. The backyard at the folks' house had a chain link fence around its border and had a huge erosion problem for years. One summer, Richard and I were driving down I-70 West near Montgomery City and spotted miles of wild daylilies growing along the highway service road. We made a mental note of the spot, and the following weekend came back with leaf bags and a shovel. That trunk full of lilies eventually lined all three sides of the back fence as they multiplied, and we divided and spread them. Every June, we had a profusion of the showy orange flowers. Each bloom lasted one day as their name suggests, but in a parade of successive buds for weeks. The piano recital for my students is always held on the last Saturday in

June, and I would bring a big bouquet of lilies to the recital hall. We could never have afforded to buy potted lilies, but sometimes nature and some effort is all we need. There is no longer any erosion.

I will miss sitting on the deck in the morning with my cup of coffee and looking across at the glorious orange blooms lining the yard. I bought a set of coffee mugs with bright yellow glaze inside, and pictures of day lilies around the outside. That will have to hold my chocolate raspberry mocha and my memories.

Did you know daylily blooms are edible? Just pull off the stamens, stuff them with cream cheese and a little salt and pepper, and fry them in a skillet with a bit of coconut oil. Amazing.

Flash forward. I drove by the old house today. It was bought by a developer who remodeled it for resale. I noticed they took out all those glorious daylilies and threw out grass seed. Now, the new owners will have erosion problems again the entire length of the fence. Stupidity wins out.

It makes me angry. I grieve for the glorious flowers ruthlessly destroyed for the ignorant obsession with grass. At my new house, I have become an avid gardener. We have terraced raised beds for vegetables, a small orchard, and flower and herb gardens. I would plow up all the grass in the front yard if the homeowner's association would allow it.

My inner child delights in its beauty and diversity. The gardens nurture my body and spirit, and I in return care for the plants. It is a symbiotic relationship. The thing the garden needs most are the footsteps of the gardener.

This spring, go to a nursery and wander among the plants. Feel which ones delight and call to you. Adopt a leaf baby. Bring one home and plant it in the yard or place a house plant on a windowsill. When we nurture and care for a plant and see it thrive, it does the same thing for our own inner child.

Gifts of the spirit are wrapped in time and truth.

New Christmas Reality— And So We Adapt

I brought an old plastic music box home, rescued from the bottom drawer in the old music studio. It is emotionally associated with most of the Christmas celebrations of my childhood.

For our family, Christmas Eve was the biggest celebration of the year. It was the one day everyone packed into my dad's older sister's home. We used to get dressed to the nines to go to auntie's house for Christmas Eve. It always seemed to be a competition to be the best dressed. My mother would take me to the big department store to try on dress after dress until the fanciest one with the most bows and ruffles was finally decided upon. It was carried home, wrapped in plastic, to hang on the back of my bedroom door as a tease until the night finally arrived when I could wear it.

We were a big group, all of Auntie's five kids who were married with children, their kids running wild through the house, the girls giggling in black patent buckle shoes and dresses with red bows, the boys with button-down collars and bow ties, and moms losing their battle to keep shirt tails tucked in. I would watch it all in overwhelmed wonder. I was never part of the pack, everyone either decades older or younger than me.

The party was always down the stairs in auntie's rec room: a big open room with linoleum floors and a built-in bar along the back wall. There was a painting of a Spanish flamenco dancer in bold black and oranges hanging behind the bar. I loved staring at her intense face and dreaming of traveling to distant lands to bring back art for the walls in my imagined future; a pursuit that still enthralls me. There was also a real bear skin hung on the north wall. I would stand in front of it and tell the bear's spirit "sorry" every time. To the right of the bar was a curio cabinet with tiny treasures from Auntie's travels to the Orient. I memorized each one. Why? Because there was nothing else to do but study the room until dinnertime. I was alone in the crowd; the adults and the packs of cousins circling around me as if I were invisible. I was always on the outside looking in.

When it was time to eat, auntie would put a cover over the pool table and we would fill it with hot covered dishes. Each of us had our assigned side dish, as predictable as the tide. My mom brought the broccoli, rice, and cheese casserole. She would make a triple batch, take two, and save one batch back for us for a much-enjoyed leftover in the week to come. My cousin would bake a huge sugar cookie covered with cream cheese, and artfully arrange it with assorted fruit slices. Another cousin would make green beans with the little crunchy onions on top. You get the idea. It was Auntie's job to bake the turkey and burn the dinner rolls. To this day I like rolls extra brown. I got used to them that way.

We would grab plastic plates and circle around the pool table, sampling the variety. I found that thrilling. My mother hated to cook. Tuna surprise and a can of green beans was about as good as it got at home. On a rare occasion, mother would fry chicken. That was wonderful, but I digress.

After dinner was the most anticipated event of the holiday and I dreaded it. Everyone got up from the rows of folding chairs and tables in front of the poor bear skin to crowd into the other side of the room where the Christmas tree stood. It was piled with presents going halfway out into the room. Cousins would descend on the pile with squeals as name tags were read and the pile was distributed. I would silently retreat to the bar to contemplate the flamenco dancer. In all those years there was only one time when a package had my name on it. One year, Auntie had a tiny music box wrapped up for me. When I turned its plastic handle a tinkling Swan Lake theme magically entwined its way into my spirit about two octaves higher than Tchaikovsky ever intended. But I was so shocked and thrilled. I vowed I would see that ballet someday, and in high school, I bought myself a ticket and went. I still have that little plastic music box, even after all these decades and many moves. It represented the one time I was noticed, which now seems equally precious and tragic.

Often, change comes in a steady flow of events so that one thing blends into the next almost seamlessly. But Christmas changed abruptly when auntie went into the nursing home and sold the house. I never see most of the cousins any more. The big group split off into smaller family pods. Each of Auntie's five children celebrates holidays now with their immediate children and grandchildren, and that is just how things logically progress. I am moving to the old folks' table. I'm not ready for it. Did I blink? How did this happen so fast?

To be sure, my parents had gifts waiting for me at home under our own tree. I remember telling my parents how disappointed I was that only Santa thought of me to bring a gift. It was his job so somehow it didn't feel special. I was just one name on a list. The next year, there were gifts with tags that read "from Mom and Dad." I liked that very much.

Now, please don't think this is about receiving gifts. It's not. It is about belonging. It is about feeling like a valued member of a family. It is about being included. I'm certain that none of my relatives had a clue how I felt, which is also kind of the point. But rather than being bitter, I learned just how important it is to be inclusive. I try to have a gift wrapped and ready for everyone who comes to my home during the holidays. My joy is making ceramic ornaments. I have glazed and fired kiln loads of handmade ornaments, each made with the recipient's name and the year painted on the back. I delight in their joy when they unwrap their treasure. It says loud and clear, "I made this especially for you. I thought of you weeks ago and spent my time and creative energy to honor you. You were not an afterthought; your gift was planned."

Being able to bring joy in this way is the gift my lonely inner child received. Without those dozens of holidays when I was left out, I would have never learned the deep truth of how important it is to include and value others.

Looking back, I can tell my inner child: You received the most lasting and precious gift of all. All the gifts that were unwrapped from under auntie's tree are long gone and forgotten, but your gift couldn't be wrapped. Your gift was timeless and has expanded outward like droplets on a lake; a lake of joy and understanding.

A joyous spirit will find a creative outlet to pour into.

Happiness—
Listen to Your Spirit Guides

I've been watching a lot of YouTube videos lately about the sun bringing our Earth and all of us humans out of the dark ages and crossing over into the new Bronze Age, the age of the awakening of the potential of the human mind and spirit. I see lots of talk about "star children" who are being marveled at and praised and encouraged to develop their extra-ordinary mental abilities. I can't help but wonder how utterly different my life path would have been if I had been nurtured and praised for my abilities instead of being shut down by glares and mocking. As an adult looking back, I was a small child who was able to see, in vivid detail, events of the past by merely touching an associated object, and on three separate occasions, I was able to see a future threat and warn of its coming, even being able to protect myself.

There were two other times that this happened. I warned my daughter of a threat on her senior trip in high school. It was a tour of Italy and Greece. I saw a small wolf pack of Italian men threatening her, but I also saw her then-boyfriend step in and back them down. He was a tall, soft-spoken vegetarian with a genuine smile and a level-five black belt. The lion purrs and lazes in the shade, but we would be fools to assume he is weak. I knew that at the moment when it snapped from teasing to serious threat, he would reveal himself capable of deadly force. And just as I had seen, the bold-in-numbers jerks backed down to seek easier prey. I heard all about it when they got home. I had already seen it.

The most recent time was while I was still living with my folks. I would teach until late in the evening, leaving the studio door open. Each student would let themselves in or out every half hour. I suddenly felt eyes of evil intent watching the door for several days in a row. Then suddenly, I felt the threat come close. I called out to my black belt almost-son and he came charging in and locked the door and stood very prominently in view through the glass door, staring back. And then I felt the eyes turn and leave. They had assumed I was alone. Thankfully, that evening I was not. They, too, slinked off in search of easier prey.

Can I prove it? Of course not. But I have a 100 percent track record.

I also hear a voice, often, and no, not like "the voices made me do it;" I mean like a guardian spirit. It can be huge things, like sitting first in line at the traffic light, it turns green, my foot goes to push on the gas pedal, and I hear "STOP" at eighty decibels. I slam on the brake, count to two, and suddenly a truck speeds through the intersection out of nowhere. Then I hear, "Take a deep breath, you're alright."

But usually, it's little everyday things, "Don't hold the carrot like that, you'll cut your finger with the peeler." Okay, thank you.

It's worse when I disobey. Like when we were in Colorado the last time. We had a favorite jewelry shop that sold handmade Native American silver and turquoise. It is a nice place run by a nice couple we had been seeing every summer for eighteen years. I had made a belly dance baby doll for their niece and gave her one of my *Friendship Flies the Sun* books. I heard the voice tell me, "Take their photo together."

I meant to, but her husband was spending a long time with another customer, and my gang was itching to leave, and I didn't get the shot. I felt strangely terrible about it. I called when we got home and learned that he had died the next day.

Or the time I was told to call my uncle in Alaska. I had never called him in my entire life. I didn't want to; he was a recluse and odd. He killed himself two weeks later. How was I supposed to know? But that is the point: it's not up to me to know. I don't need to know if I am open to doing things for others that I may not be comfortable with.

The photo was for the wife, not me. The call was to become aware that the uncle needed help and intervention. Not for me, for them.

I try so hard to do the kind things I am prompted to do, and they are always kind. Often, I argue. Like this Christmas, I was urged to make ornaments for an additional five children. I argue, "I don't have time," and I get back, "Then stay up all night. Make time."

I argue, "They won't be appreciated," and I hear, "That is not your concern."

So, I stayed up all night. I needed to do it for them, not recognition for my efforts. There is a huge difference.

I say all of this to explore this thought. What if we all stop suppressing our instincts to perform random acts of kindness? What if we embrace the spiritual talents we possess? What if we actively try to exercise our latent abilities, like seeing events behind or in front of our seeming place on the timeline? What if we all look at each human as a being of endless value and potential? Is it too late for me to heighten my own awareness? Or has the perspective of a longer timeline of experience been the missing element I needed?

I was recently talking to someone about an incident in which I had felt used and, quite frankly, abused. Their response upset me at the time. They said, "Only you can make yourself happy."

I understand that. Happiness is a state of consciousness we choose. Things cannot make us happy, but a joyful spirit can enjoy the beauty of the arts more fully. Work cannot cause you to be fulfilled, but a joyous spirit will find a creative outlet to pour into, and every task will bring a gratification to purpose. A joyous spirit will flower in their relationships because they place genuine value on those relationships. They will attract positive, creative people to themselves. If I believe everyone that I talk to is interesting and of value, they are.

Case in point, I noticed the girls that sit behind the bank desk at the grocery store get walked past by hundreds of gloomy shoppers every day. Dull people stand in line to do their banking in a rush to check out and get to their next task. The bank clerk is merely a speed bump. I started really looking at each teller. All are young women, of all races, all with different accents and distinctive dress styles and hairdos. I started making a point of making eye contact and smiling and asking them a simple question about themselves. Something like, "I'm going to the art fair this weekend. Do you have any plans?"

They light up. The floodgates open, and over time I know all about each one of them. They have children and interests and are pursuing degrees. They, in turn, ask about how my trip was and want to see pictures of my grandchildren. We smile. It turns out they are all valuable, interesting people. We look forward to seeing each other, and it has been a blessing for me; a little beam of light in the middle of a hectic day. We can always count on a moment of being real, valuable human beings. It's a breath of fresh air. What if we all tried to be caring and positive in all of our interactions? The ripples would flow out in all directions.

It's 1:00 a.m. So, on that note, I think I'll go take melatonin and try to get some sleep. Maybe more tomorrow if the muse hits.

Now, it's 6:30 a.m. I just woke up and realized why I got upset. While it is true that "only you can make yourself happy," it is never acceptable to use that as an excuse for treating others unjustly or callously. We are still equally responsible for our own actions towards others.

HAPPINESS—LISTEN TO YOUR SPIRIT GUIDES

And so, after all these years, I understand happiness is more of a pursuit than a destination. It's the blossom on the tree of life. It's up to each of us to nurture and protect. To be creative. To contribute and learn and grow and adapt. To be kind and compassionate. We can tell our inner child that they are safe, and it is finally their turn to thrive.

The spirit manifests the physical.

She Cut Her Hair — Manifest Reality

Until about an hour ago, I used to love listening to a favorite pop singer of mine. I had YouTube scrolling through videos of her performances and was enthralled with the purity and passion of the vocals. Then one image of her jarred me. OMG, she dyed her hair lighter! How awful. She still has long glorious curls, but my artist's eye picked up immediately on a lighter shade of brown; kind of a non-descript medium brown, not the decadent chocolate of her natural hair. It was flat and lifeless. I said out loud, "I'd hate the person who did that to me."

Then, a song later, my eyes were scarred forever. Her luxurious brown tresses were massacred, chopped off and died the ugliest fake blonde I had ever seen. I turned off the TV and threw the remote. My husband said, "She is just a kid playing with her hair."

"It will grow back," you may ask? Perhaps not.

In my senior year of high school, I got a job singing and dancing in the Palace Show at Six Flags Over Mid-America. I danced six shows a day in 110-degree heat, and as a result, I was wringing wet with sweat at the end of every day. The backstage and the dressing room had no air conditioning. We used to open the refrigerator and stand in front of it to try to cool off. My hair had never been cut and my tresses were below my knees. It took two hours a day to wash and dry, and I was doing it every night when I got home at 9 p.m. after dancing six shows and an hour's drive home. I made the decision to cut my hair to my shoulder blades.

When I came home, my father broke down and cried. Dad used to call me Troll, after the little plastic dolls with tiny bodies and twice as much hair. I had a whole collection of the dolls that I played with as a child. I took it as a negative that he did not like my long hair. The tears were a shock.

I found that set of troll dolls in the toy closet as I emptied the house. I had saved them from my childhood to pass down. My daughter didn't really play with them, and now they have gotten sticky as the plastic breaks down with age. I'll have to say goodbye to the troll dolls, and my nickname.

My hair has never grown any longer than my shoulder blades since. No matter how many years I go between haircuts, it remembers and refuses to grow a centimeter longer than the first cut. I thank God I didn't go any shorter. I've been trying to grow it out

for over forty years, to no avail. There are decisions we make in our youth that carry forward.

Youth and beauty are fleeting, but only of the body, not of the soul. I forgive myself for cutting my hair. It was a practical solution to a stressful situation. I let myself grieve consequences for years. Now, however, I realize that we fret over things that ultimately do not matter. I met and married my husband Richard, and he loves me. He doesn't care how long my hair is or isn't. He would love me even if I were bald.

I used to wear stiletto heels and sequins. Now it's tennis shoes and T-shirts. He doesn't care what I wear. We are comfortable with our relationship.

Now, I can tell my inner child that most of what had upset me will not matter in the end.

*If you listen long enough,
people will reveal their true identity.*

The Mink Coat—
I've Come a Long Way

When I was in grade school, my parents rarely went out. My dad was always "working late" or gone "fixing an apartment," or "at the library," which apparently took from 6 a.m. to midnight Saturday and Sunday. But once in a great while, there would be a wedding to go to and they would get dressed up and go. I have a vivid image in my mind of my mother with her hair up in a tight French roll and putting her full-length mink coat on as they left, and I remember thinking how pretty she could be. From that moment on, I associated being pretty with that coat.

Fast forward. We moved my parents out of their house and into the assisted living apartment. I never saw the coat. I didn't ask about it.

My husband and I visit the folks for lunch almost every Sunday and then sit and talk to them for a couple of hours. Our entire Sunday afternoon is given over to them nearly every week. It's a big sacrifice. With Richard working 7 a.m. to 5 p.m. and me working 3 p.m. to 9 p.m., we get very little time together. By the time I'm done teaching, I'm really spent. The children have sucked all the energy out of me. It's just on the weekend we reconnect.

Yesterday, my mom started by saying she tried to get my daughter to wear her mink to my cousin's wedding two weeks ago, but she didn't want to. She said she would not wear fur. Then Mom said, "I tried to think of which nurse to give it to, but they are all too fat and I don't think it would fit any of them. So, if you want to try it on, you can."

Wow! Does she even hear herself? What a lousy thing to say! I'm so low on the list that any hired caregiver in the place would be preferable to her only child? I used to get fighting mad when things like this happened, but these days I just feel sorry for them.

I have three beautiful furs we have bought over the years. I don't need her coat. But it would have been so nice to be able to feel that happy childhood memory. Now I will never wear it because it will forever be a reminder of just how low I am in her eyes. I'm expected to do all the work, but never loved or appreciated. It's just her guilty conscience that made her give me the coat instead of donating it to Goodwill. I will, however, sell it at some point, and at least get back some of the gas money we spend driving to their place forty minutes away.

As we are walking out the door, my dad waves me over to him. I'm thinking, oh good, maybe he will say he really wants me to have the coat and that will negate some of my mother's negative speech. But what comes out of his mouth? "I paid $3,000 for that coat decades ago, so it's probably worth $6,000 by now. So, if she (my daughter) ever indicates she wants it, you give it to her immediately!" Sigh. I should have known.

Another thought I had is that everything I own I have already mentally, emotionally, and legally willed to my daughter. Happily. I am proud I have something to give her, and I hope she will be happy to have things to remember me by to support and promote the family into future generations. That the concept of passing down your wealth to your child is so far outside of their thinking that they would feel the need to demand I do this is mind-blowing.

THE MINK COAT—I'VE COME A LONG WAY

In an odd way, I'm truly glad this entire exchange took place. It is an affirmation of just how far I have come on my healing journey.

Their arrows now drop to the ground without hitting their mark. I just sigh and shake my head and move on. I can love my parents and continue to help and support them the best way I am able and separate these things as an unfortunate manifestation of their own hurt and problems. We will still do our best to take them on the annual trip to Colorado and add as much joy as we are able to their lives. It is possible to love them, but not love what they do.

I can hear my father yelling at me just weeks before their move to the nursing home, "I wish you had never been born. You were the only reason I stayed with her!" (meaning my mother).

I was shocked at the time. Now, it carries no emotional impact at all.

I love myself. I love my inner child. I am grateful and blessed in the life and relationships I have cultivated.

I can create in the flow of positive energy. My Divine Creator has sent angels to guide and protect me. I know every soul is loved and valuable. Even yours, mom and dad. Even if you don't know it.

Time is an illusion. We can remember the future.

Slippers—
Three Pairs, Three Journeys

Apparently, it's possible to remember the future. I've been confused about this since last Christmas, more precisely since Thursday, December 20. I should be precise since the topic is, after all, time.

My favorite piano students are a brother and sister, aged ten and twelve, who come on Thursdays for their weekly piano lesson. Their mother is our best friend's daughter and we have known the entire family, all the children and grandchildren, for decades now.

As the two walked in they were grinning ear to ear, and the sister was holding a package behind her back. "Merry Christmas!" they said as they presented into my hands a crinkled mess of a wrapped gift that had obviously been wrapped, opened, and rewrapped.

My mind took a lurch, like hitting a speed bump, and I flashed a memory of this same package being handed to me and I thought, "just like last year." They giggled "open it!" and again the memory of "that's what happened last year," echoed in my mind.

I opened the double tape on tape to reveal the exact pair of slippers they had given me last year. They were a distinctive plaid with purple as the dominant color. I remembered last year looking at the tag and it read "to Aunt Mimi." My mind was spinning, I looked at the tag and it read "to Aunt Mimi," and the sister blushed red and said, "I reused the paper," which was the exact thing she said in my memory, in the exact way, instant replay.

I remembered thinking, "it's a re-gift," and glancing at the size marked 10-12. I know their Aunt Mimi, and she would need size 12 slippers, but these fit me. I remembered all this, every detail, and every thought, from last year, I thought. And I remembered thinking, "these were obviously mis-marked and didn't fit Mimi, so I got them."

No matter, I really like them and will wear them. I thought this exact same sequence all before. I know you can just casually say "déjà vu," but I also remember wearing these slippers for months and months and I distinctly remember being sad when I finally threw them away, having worn them out completely. I remember sitting at the edge of the bed staring at the frayed heels, completely crushed.

This has been haunting me every day since December 20. It's now February 24, oh, now it's 12:04 a.m. so February 25, and I'm writing this all down. I've been looking around the house for an old pair of these slippers, thinking maybe I still have the worn-out twin, and feeling confused. I finally got up the courage to ask my husband as we went through our bedtime routines, "Have you ever seen these slippers before? Do you remember me wearing a pair just like this till I wore them out?"

He says, "No, I've never seen another pair, you just got these."

So, then I was obligated to go through this lame explanation for him as well. And he said, predictably, "It's just déjà vu," (like anyone knows what that really is either. Just because someone stuck a name on it doesn't negate or explain anything).

So how can I also remember hundreds of times putting them on and mourning their being thrown away, used up? In this timeline, I'm not caught up to that yet. Did I loop back? Was I sent backward, and that little bit of memory didn't get erased? Is this a "take two," and am I supposed to be doing something differently this time through? Or does everything occur simultaneously, and I slipped over a track for a bit? Why does it play back like a memory and not a prediction? And who the heck cares about an old pair of slippers anyway? Couldn't I have seen a slice of the future a bit more interesting or profound? Anyway, I like these slippers.

Which reminds me of another pair of slippers. My pair of solid purple slippers I wore out last year (I think) had a button with several sparkly crystals sewn on the sides. My granddaughter, now three, loves crystals, so before I threw out my old pair, I snipped off the buttons. I wrapped them in Christmas paper and put them in the toe of her stocking. She was thrilled when she opened them. I told her I would sew them on the sides of her slippers, and she did a little joy dance. I did just that while she was taking her nap, setting them by her bed. When she walked out from her nap, she was wearing her newly jeweled slippers, beaming with happiness. "Thank you, Grammie, now they will remind me of you and make me happy." I will hold that gift in my heart.

Today, I found an entire box full of crinkled, fading Polaroid photos of black and white scenes of Alaska. I literally pulled it out of the attic, balancing on a ladder and straining to get it through the trap door in the garage above the kitchen.

Which reminds me of a third pair of slippers. My mother had a younger brother. I only met him once that I remember, but I grew up hearing about him and seeing photographs of him. He was only a few months younger than my mother, and I heard stories about their childhood. Apparently, my mother thought she could boss him like a second mother when they were kids, and he was not having it. He didn't talk until he was almost three, and then it was to tell my mom off!

SLIPPERS—THREE PAIRS, THREE JOURNEYS

Mom said he would sneak outside at night and scratch at her bedroom window to scare her. I remember seeing his photo. He was a young skinny teenager with flaming red hair and freckles, just like his dad when he was young. He went to Kansas University just a year behind my mom. I was shown a photo of him and his date and my mom and her date, who was my dad, having a Coke at the Blue Moon dance hall. He, like my dad, fought in Korea, but Mom said he fell in love with a Korean girl and wanted to marry her. He called my mom and told her, and she told him that she and his mother would never accept her and to find an American girl. He swore if he couldn't marry her, he would never marry.

By the time I came along, he was living in Nome, Alaska, six months out of the year, and living at the White Alice site the other six months. He had gotten a degree in electrical engineering and was maintaining the White Alice satellite relay station that was so remote that they had to drop food and supplies in by plane. He was a complete hermit, living six months of each year in complete isolation. His only neighbors, if you could call them that, were the occasional Eskimos that passed through. He would send a photo now and again of his car buried in snow. He had dug a trench under his car so he could light a fire under it to thaw it out enough to start it.

Well, one Christmas, a box arrived wrapped in brown paper from Alaska. It had a pair of seal-skin Eskimo slippers with a beaded flower medallion on each toe. "For Ann from Uncle." Wow! What a treasure! I loved them so much! I wore them until my toes poked through the ends and they fell apart. I cut the beaded medallions off and kept them in my jewelry box. I had them for years. I wonder if I still have them in a drawer somewhere. I'll have to search for them.

The one time he came to visit us, I was in grade school. He came in January and complained it was too hot. It was zero degrees outside.

He was used to fifty below. I remember he was a sickly, pale man with graying hair, chain-smoking as he sat on the brown couch in the living room. I watched astonished as he lit one cigarette with another.

I remember being so disappointed. How could this unhealthy, bitter person be the one who had sent me such a treasure? They just did not match.

True to his words, he never married. Mom said he went to Alaska to get as far away from the family as he could. He got esophagus cancer and eventually couldn't swallow; that is, except for the gun he finally took his life with. I always wondered why he didn't marry her anyway.

Here's the weird thing. I was recovering from the knee surgery I told you about, sitting with my leg in a whirlpool bath at physical therapy, when I heard a voice say "call your uncle" in my head. How random, right? I had never had a conversation with him. He had never been a part of our lives. Even the phone calls to my mom had stopped years and years ago. He hadn't attended my wedding, nothing, so I didn't do it, and I felt guilty, but I just didn't want to. I didn't know him.

My mom got a phone call two weeks later from the sheriff in Nome. Her brother had committed suicide that morning. Could a phone call from me have changed his course? I'll never know. But more importantly, where did the voice come from? I believe it is guidance from my spirit guides.

Someone knew what he was planning and wanted me to intervene. Could I have cured his cancer? Of course not. But perhaps I could have helped comfort his spirit.

I had started collecting Alaska-themed Christmas ornaments. Each year a new one came out, with a little Eskimo and a seal or walrus or some such thing. I'm not sure why I wanted to collect them except they reminded me of how thrilled I was with those slippers. They go on my Christmas tree every year, but my uncle never knew about them.

SLIPPERS—THREE PAIRS, THREE JOURNEYS

Mom had him buried next to his parents in Augusta, Kansas, where they grew up. So much for being as far away from family as possible.

Now, as an adult, I can see that he had chosen to stop living years ago. He listened to the words of negative hurtful rejection, and never gave himself permission to follow his own heart. All lives have pivotal moments. Angry, hateful words sling like arrows from the very people we look to for compassion. But it is up to us where those arrows land. Raise your shield and march forward. Give yourself permission to love who you will. Give yourself permission to thrive and rejoice in the fullness of this experience we call life.

I will thank my uncle now for the gift that brought my inner child joy and raise my shield.

When I hear the arrow of angry, limiting words hurled at me in memory, I can smile and enfold my inner child. You are safe. You can thrive in the love and creative flow of the universe. You are limitless.

P.S. It is 2:00 a.m. and I just found the beaded medallions still in a drawer in my jewelry box. Now I can go to bed, except I probably won't be able to sleep. My feet are ice cold. I've been sitting here all this time and forgot to put on my slippers. I know, right?!

Parting Thoughts

I'll start by saying I finally caved to curiosity and drove a mile and half from my house back to see the old house of my childhood. Every tree in the front yard, every ivy vine, every daffodil bulb and perennial flower have been scoured away. An empty flat space of grass stares back. The spirits of the land weep. Even the majestic hackberry tree has been attacked by chainsaws.

And so, it's time to walk away.

Thank you for traveling with me on this journey that we all must eventually embark upon. It is a bittersweet experience to transition aging parents. Make the best of it. Take away what you need, let go of the rest.

Is there a child within who is still looking for approval from family members who are incapable of giving it? The child who wants approval is never going to get it except from themselves. Longing for approval can be a hard task to master. It can push us to strive for better grades in school, higher goals, and achievements. It can be a motivator toward greater success. However, we need to give ourselves permission to enjoy these achievements without the external approval our inner child longs for. Come to peace with the realization that the only one who can give you approval is you. Learn to enjoy those successes and goals met in the present moment. Celebrate, or you will forever be chasing after the next award on an exhausting treadmill of unattainable acceptance. The only one in life I want to impress for the rest of my life is my inner child. Impressing everyone else is exhausting. I check in with her and ask: how am I doing? Did I laugh today? Did I give others my full undivided attention? Did I love unconditionally? Did I create a safe space for others?

Love yourself. Love your inner child.

Sometimes the best way to move forward is to pause and look back.

There are many other stories to be told, to be sure. There was the bird that called for help, the deer that kissed us, the little red broom, the ring made from a peach seed, the petrified snake head, the painted pot, the mouse holding the hourglass, and so it goes. Perhaps there is still much to unpack. But I will leave those musings for another day.

Acknowledgments

Ah! It's done. First and foremost, I'd like to thank all the beta readers: Michael, Pat, Monica, Domnic, and Sampada. Thank you for your constructive feedback that helped me get these stories out to the world.

To my Steve Harrison editing and production team, I stand and applaud you. Because of you, my manuscript is polished and ready for the world to see.

To David Bentley for the cover photo. Your artistry is unmatched.

To my husband Richard. Thank you for your steadfast presence and support. Thank you for loving all of me, my inner child and my still evolving adult self.

My Mission is to teach mindfulness and compassion to the children of the world and to the child that still lives within each of us. To offer healing from childhood trauma and send self-love and acceptance back in time to your inner child.

> *My mission is to empower each of us to send love and self-acceptance to the child that still lives within. To find the grace of forgiveness, the wisdom to learn from adversity, the courage to confront your memories, the resilience to move forward with confidence, the faith in the eternal love of the universe.*

How you can help:

1. Post an honest review on Amazon.

2. Send a screenshot of the review to ann@annmracek.com and I will send you a free bonus chapter, Practical Steps to Unpacking the Attic (Overwhelmed to Empty Walls).

About the Author

Ann Mracek has always been the keeper of her own calendar, expressing her creative flow through a kaleidoscope of entrepreneurial adventures.

She is the author of *My Best Friends Live in the Woods: The Adventures of Albert*. Albert Raccoon is adopted by Mother Skunk in an enchanted forest. Each chapter teaches concepts of mindfulness and compassion in a fun interactive way, followed by discussion and questions to encourage meaningful conversation. As storyteller, illustrator, and composer, she is producing this novel as a series of videos on YouTube at *My Best Friends Live in the Woods*.

Ann was the director of Aabla Raqs (mirror dance) Belly Dance Company. Under this umbrella, she was principal dancer, choreographer, teacher, and composer of dance music, as well as the costume and set designer. She is author of the children's book, *Friendship Flies the Sun: The Ancient Egyptian Legend of Scarab Beetle*, which the dance company performed as an interactive stage show at schools and Renaissance faires.

She has been a singer and dancer at Six Flags Over Mid America, the lead in many musicals, and a singer in a popular event band. She also founded Mracek Studio in 1979, where she still teaches piano, voice, and music composition.

Ann has her bachelor's and master's degrees in music theory composition from the University of Kansas, having earned both degrees in four years.

She composes for her beloved instrument, the piano, almost daily.

Recordings and scores of her Symphony No. 1 Shadow Dragon, chamber works, piano, and piano/vocal compositions are available on her website: https://www.mybestfriendsliveinthewoods.com.

Ann has one grown daughter and two adored grandchildren. She lives with her husband Richard in Saint Louis, Missouri. Avid travelers, their exuberant love of adventure and passion for cultures has had them in twenty-two countries in the past thirteen years: many multiple times. As world citizens, our shared humanity is best expressed through compassion.

Her unique experiences as both teacher and creator combine with humor and insight to make her a masterful storyteller and an excellent speaker.

To contact the author, please send an email to: annmracek@annmracek.com

More information is available at https://annmracek.com

www.ingramcontent.com/pod-product-compliance
Lightning Source LLC
Chambersburg PA
CBHW051948290426
44110CB00015B/2153